My Hightov

1897 - 1969

being personal reminiscences

by

Joe Bulman

3rd edition, revised and enlarged

by

Andrew Lee-Hart and Matthew Tinker

SEFTON
LIBRARIES

Published by Sefton Council
Leisure Services Department (Libraries)
Pavilion Buildings, 99-105 Lord Street
Southport PR8 1RH

First edition 1975
Second (revised) edition 1990
Third (revised & enlarged) edition 2003

ISBN 1-874516-10-3

Printed in Great Britain by Poplar Services Printers Limited

CONTENTS

		page
List of illustrations		iv
Introduction		v
Acknowledgements		vi
Chapter 1	Earliest memories and growth	1
Chapter 2	Hightown Hotel	9
Chapter 3	Truant School	14
Chapter 4	Voluntary Fire Brigade	19
Chapter 5	St. Stephen's Church	24
Chapter 6	Our Lady of Victories RC Church	29
Chapter 7	Crosby Lighthouse	33
Chapter 8	Hightown Club	35
Chapter 9	Land drainage	38
Chapter 10	River Alt and coastal areas	42
Chapter 11	The Railway	49
Chapter 12	The Estate	51
Chapter 13	Footpath to Formby	54
Appendix 1	Footpaths dispute	56
Appendix 2	Hightown miscellany	60
Appendix 3	The Hightown War Memorial	64
Appendix 4	The Hightown Club Roll of Honour	70
Appendix 5	Hightown Club	74
Appendix 6	Fort Crosby	76
Appendix 7	The Truant School	78
Appendix 8	P.C. Bond	83
Bibliography		85

LIST OF ILLUSTRATIONS

		collection	page
Map 1	Hightown c1846	C: M780	vi
Map 2	Hightown 1927	C: M743 + M740	viii
1.	Joe Bulman	C: PE54	1
2.	Group, early 1920s	Mrs Page	2
3.	Alt Road	[Cushing] Col.Bryson	2
4.	Farm Dairy, Sandy Lane	Mrs Rutherford	4
5.	Pharmacy, School Road, c1931	Mrs Owen	4
6.	Sunday School Outing, c1927	Lieut-Col.Cook / Mrs Neale	6
7.	War Memorial (sand dunes)	Mrs Owen	10
8.	Gaffney's Store, in snow	C: PA10/71	10
9.	Village Green, early 1930s	C: OD/HIG1	12
10.	Truant School	S: P25/2	15
11.	View from Truant School	Mrs Owen	17
12.	Great Crosby Fire Brigade 1907	C: FB2	20
13.	Great Crosby Fire Brigade 1920	C: FB3	20
14.	Hightown Stores, formerly Gaffney's, 1992	Lieut-Col.Cook	22
15.	St. Stephen's Church, exterior	Mrs Owen	24
16.	St. Stephen's Church, Bishop's visit	C: OD/HIG-CHA4 [Crosby Herald]	26
17.	Pantomime group, 1920s	Mrs Neale	26
18.	Our Lady of Victories Church, interior	S: P25/8	30
19.	Our Lady of Victories, Archbishop's visit	C: OD/HIG-CHR3 [Crosby Herald]	30
20.	Altcar Grange	Col.Bryson	31
21.	Crosby Lighthouse	Col.Bryson	33
22.	P.C. Bond	Col.Bryson	34
23.	"Ingleside", Sandy Lane	Lieut-Col.Cook	35
24.	Hightown Club, tennis courts	Mrs Owen	36
25.	"Near Altcar" by J.H.Williams	[The Walker] Col.Bryson	39
26.	Hightown Pumping Station	D.Corkish	40
27.	Submerged forest	C: OD/HIG-SF6	43
28.	Coastal erosion, Blundellsands	C: CO51 (right)	45
29.	Railway Station	S: P25/4	49
30.	Bridge construction works	Col.Bryson	50
31.	"The Luff" house	Mr & Mrs Perkins	52
32.	Lower Alt Road	Mrs Owen	53
33.	Hightown Cross	C: CROH1 [Manchester Library]	54
34.	War Memorial	C: OD/HIG-WM1	61
35.	Remembrance Day 1968	C: OD/HIG-WM2 [Crosby Herald]	61
36.	Fort Crosby, c1950	K.Bargen	76
37.	Fort Crosby, March 1957	C: FTC2 [Crosby Herald]	77
38.	Truant School	S: P25/1	82
39.	FUN 123	Mrs Hinde	86
40.	Aerial view of Hightown	[Southport Visiter] Mrs Page	inside back cover

Reference codes in the above list relate to the Local History collections at Crosby [C] and Southport [S] Libraries

INTRODUCTION

"My Hightown" by Joe Bulman was originally published by Sefton Libraries in 1975, then edited and reissued in 1990. It became an important local history resource for the village of Hightown, but has been out of print for many years. As a result of its continued popularity it was decided to produce a new edition. The original (1990) text of this personal reminiscence has been retained; however, our research has enabled us to add new photographs and appendices.

Joe Bulman was born in 1890, in Everton, Liverpool. From the age of six he went regularly to Hightown with his father, a builder, who was restoring the floodgate bridge at Altcar Rifle Range; and also to visit a relative who lived in the village. In 1903 or 1904 the Bulman family came to live in School Road, Hightown and Joe lived there for the rest of the life, except when serving in the forces during the 1st World War.

When Joe first visited Hightown it was a relatively new community. It came into existence as a village in the 1880s, being located by the Liverpool-Southport railway line. In 1896, when Joe first knew it, there were ten cottages, four houses, Gaffney's shop, the old pub, the Hightown Hotel, the Truant School – and lots of sand. Even by the 1900s Hightown only had one paved road (Alt Road). During Joe's lifetime Hightown expanded rapidly: the book traces this growth, and Joe's views on it.

Joe, with his father and two brothers (Jack and Jim) contributed greatly to the development of Hightown. They were house builders and were responsible for constructing many of the older houses, including those on School Road, Lower Alt Road, Thornbeck Avenue, St. Stephen's Road, Hester Close, Sandy Lane and Elmcroft Lane. After the death of his second brother, Jim, in 1968 (Jack had died in a boating accident in the 1920s, on a Good Friday), Joe and his nephew Robert Parr continued in the building trade, albeit in a minor way.

Joe became affectionately known as 'Mr Hightown', due to his knowledge of the village and his involvement in its affairs. He died in January 1981 at the age of 90. Despite the intervening twenty years or so, many in Hightown still remember him well and have many anecdotes to tell about him.

Any book of reminiscences will be idiosyncratic. Joe had his particular interests – especially worrying about the danger of flooding, to the extent that he kept a boat in his shed in case of emergencies. As Joe's nephew, Arthur Parr, said in his foreword to the 1990 edition "That Joe was concerned in the development of Hightown from a very early age – although not always to his satisfaction – is clearly shown in these most interesting and very readable recollections." This book is, indeed, an informative history of Hightown, its people and institutions.

Andrew Lee-Hart & Matthew Tinker
September 2003

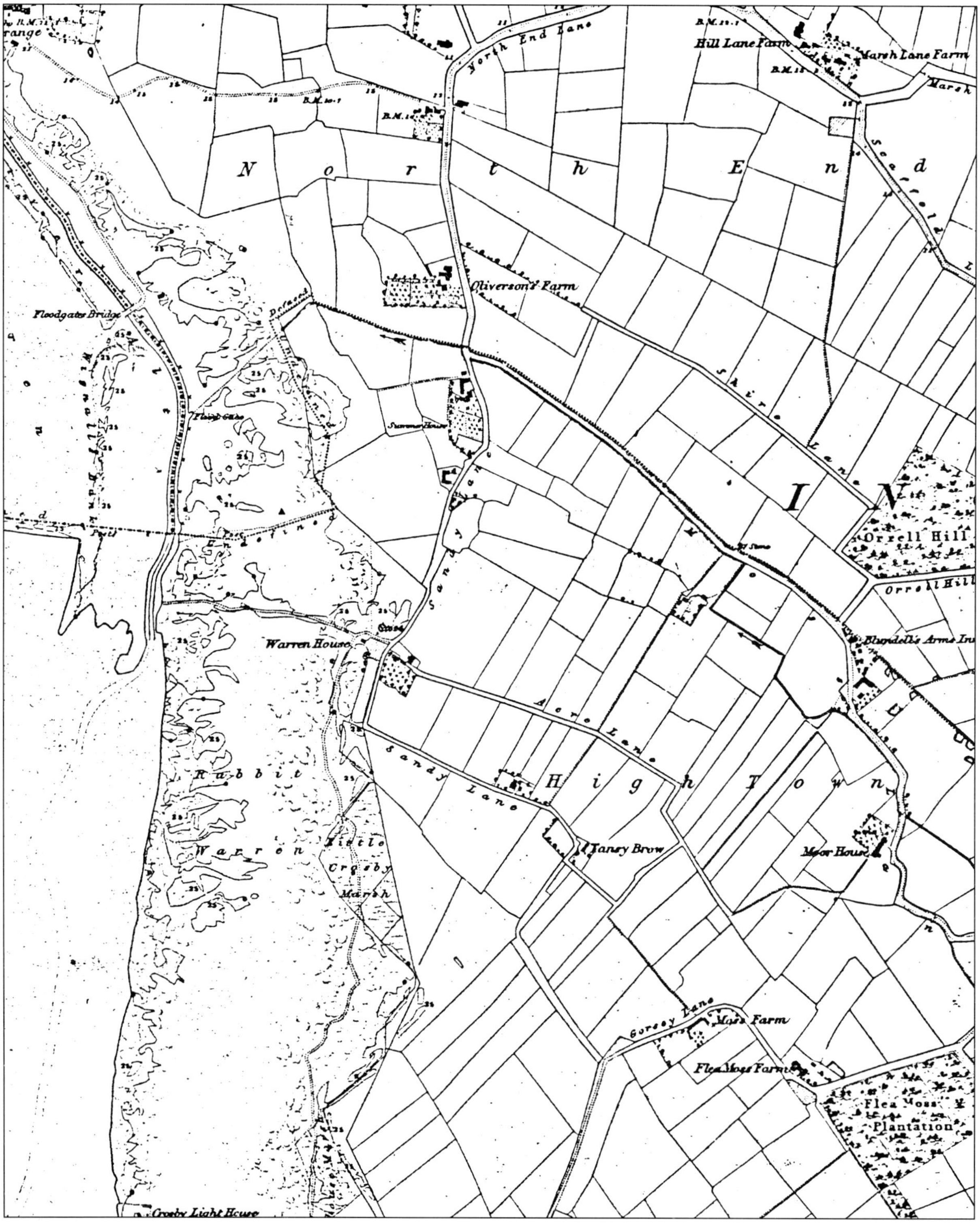

Hightown c1846
(Ordnance Survey 6" - 1 mile)

ACKNOWLEDGEMENTS

A project such as this involves many people behind the scenes. Our first debt, however, is to Mrs Elspeth Thornton, Joe Bulman's great-niece, who gave us permission to reissue "My Hightown".

Without the unstinting help and co-operation of all our contacts, we would not have been able to include the numerous 'extras' in this new edition: Mr & Mrs Bailey; Reverend John Baker; Kevin Bargen; Colonel J.Graeme Bryson; Daz Corkish; the late Lieutenant-Colonel Michael Cook; Ian Cowell; Hal Giblin; Mrs Phyll Hinde; Mrs Betty Neale; Mrs Dilys Owen; Mrs Mavis Page; Mr & Mrs Perkins; Mrs Margaret Rutherford; Mr Philip & the late Mrs Audrey Winter. Thank you for your patience during our endless questioning and numerous visits – we hope you think it was worth the effort.

We are grateful to the following for permission to include items, or for valuable assistance in research: the *Crosby Herald*, especially Chris Hannaway; the Cushing Collection (Anthony Cushing); Lancashire Record Office; Liverpool Record Office; Manchester Archives & Local Studies (Manchester Central Library), especially Paula Moorhouse; National Museums, Liverpool (The Walker), especially Audrey Hall and Moira Lindsay; the *Southport Visiter*.

Finally, to our colleagues Andrew Farthing, Alice Ronson and Mark Sargant in Sefton Libraries' Local History Service – who have all lived with this project for so long – many thanks for your tolerance.

Sefton Libraries: Local History Service

South Sefton:
Crosby Library, Crosby Road North, Waterloo L22 0LQ
Tel: 0151 257 6401
E-mail: local-history.south@leisure.sefton.gov.uk

North Sefton:
Southport Library, Lord Street, Southport PR8 1DJ
Tel: 0151 934 2119
E-mail: local-history.north@leisure.sefton.gov.uk

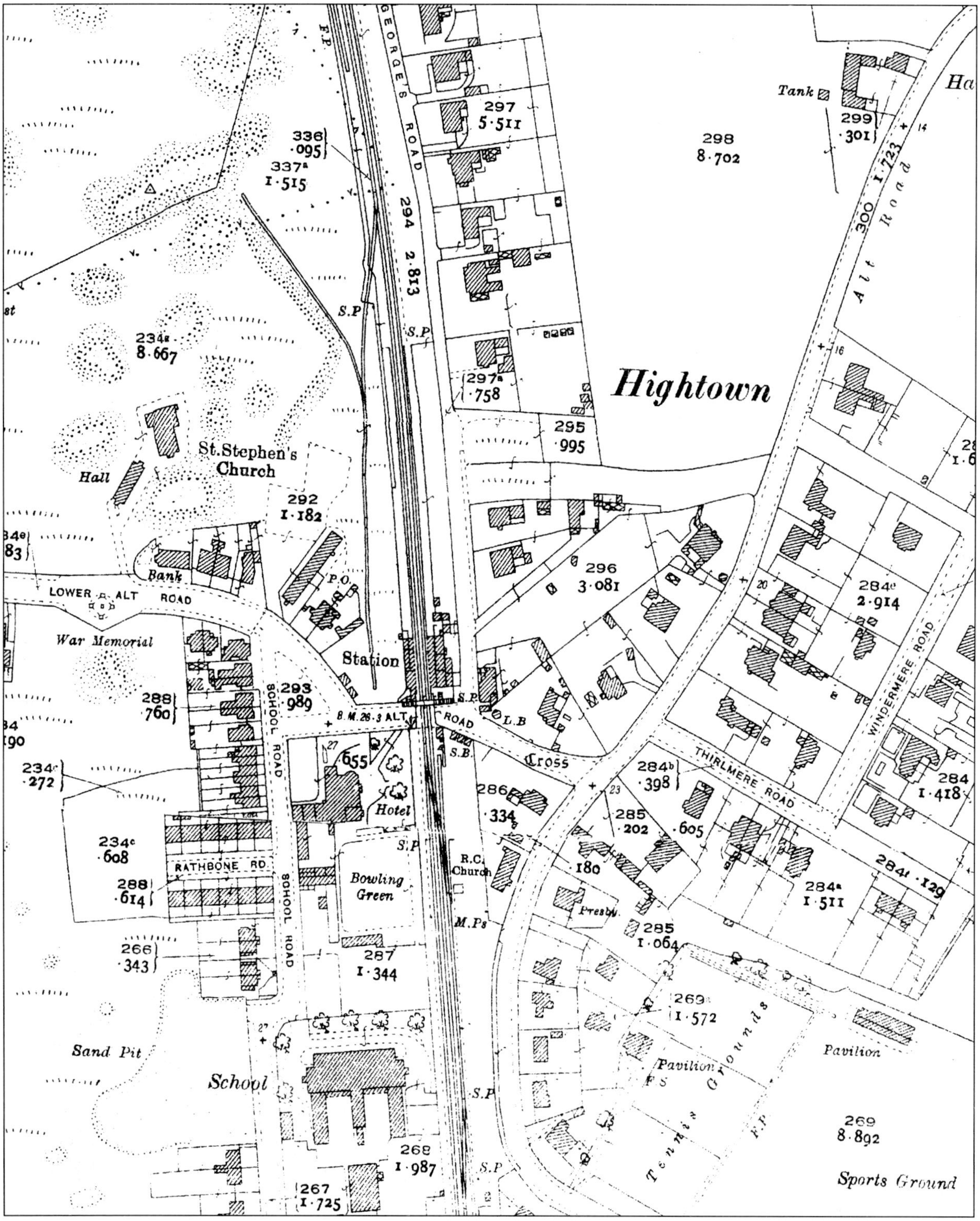

Hightown c1927
(Ordnance Survey 25" - 1 mile)

CHAPTER ONE

Earliest memories and growth

My earliest recollections of Hightown go back to the period 1896 and 1897 when my father was restoring the floodgate bridge at Altcar Rifle Range, refacing the brickwork and installing two pairs of new oak gates. We lived at that time in North Liverpool close to Everton Football Club and, during the progress of the work on the bridge, he took me with him on several occasions. A look at the O.S. map for 1891 gives a good indication of the size and extent of our village of the period, and it did not alter until 1904. The shore side of the railway consisted only of the Hotel and Truant School, four cottages opposite the school in School Road (which were originally intended for married quarters for truant school staff) and two railway cottages in what is now Lower Alt Road facing the village green. On what is now the site of the War Memorial stood the old mortuary. My elder brother Jack and myself were called on many times in those early days to give our local policeman a helping hand to remove a body from the shore and transfer it to the mortuary. Most of the victims of the Isle of Man Steamship *Ellan Vanin*, which broke its back off the Bar Lightship about 1908, floated up on our shore and we were commandeered by the Police to give a hand. The only other building on this side of the railway was the Crosby Lighthouse which was burned out in February 1898 with the loss of the Keeper, his wife and one visitor and also a large collie type dog.

The rest of this side of the railway was just covered with massive sandhills. The site where my house stands at present was occupied by a huge sandhill from the top of which you could look over the hotel roof, and another smaller hill was situated where the village green now stands. School Road was roughly pitched (I expect for access to the Truant School) but was covered with blown sand, and the hotel boundary wall adjacent to the wine shop was buried beneath the sand, so much so that in February 1898 when the lighthouse was on fire, the horse-drawn Crosby Fire Brigade could get no further than a few yards clear of the level crossing gates. Lower Alt Road was just a sandy track to the River Alt and was originally the filled-up excavation after the laying of the sewer pipes to the outfall at the river. All tides above 28 feet washed up this track as far as the War Memorial, but of

1. Joe Bulman (1890-1981)
This photo was taken towards the end of his life, and was used as the front cover of the 1990 edition of 'My Hightown'

2. Group, early 1920s
The photo shows a bungalow in the sand hills, prior to the building of Riverside and Thornbeck Avenue. Jack Bulman, brother of Joe, is in the back row, third from right. Isaac Jones, father of Mavis Page, is wearing a bowtie and is seated on the right.

3. Alt Road
An early view from the studio of Stephen S. Cushing, Crosby. Alt Road was the first paved thoroughfare in the village. Straight ahead is the level crossing and station. A horse-drawn cart, loaded with goods in sacks, is just rounding the bend.

course this track was at least 4 feet lower than the surfaced roadway as at present. When Cammell Lairds were launching the battle cruisers *Lion*, *Tiger*, etc., about 1908 onwards, huge logs floated up the track and pedestrians had to climb up the adjacent sandhills if they wanted to pass until the logs were carted away.

It must be remembered, however, that there were no sandhills on the Rifle Range side of the river until after the 1918 War and the shore extended on the Range side for about 60 or 70 yards nearer Formby. Consequently, a big tide had full access and with a west wind behind it forced all flotsam up the bottle neck of the track which is now Lower Alt Road. The big bend in the river at this period was not as pronounced as at present and it started at the yacht slipway and took a southwesterly direction before turning to Hall Road. Mark Road, St. Stephen's Road, Thornbeck Avenue and Riverside were just big sandhills. There was a bit of clearing at what is now Rathbone Road and on the clearing were a couple of wooden loose boxes used by hotel patrons' horses and a large open wooden shed which provided cover for four or five horse broughams. No doubt this clearing was made when the hotel was built, and the sand used on the building and for filling up. Blundell Road was just a cart track alongside the Truant School fence and finished approximately at "Lyndhurst" where, as well as giving access to the hotel's asparagus plantation, and the pigeon shooting field, it turned towards the shore on what is now the site of a new garage for the house "Lyndhurst". Then it wound through a rift in the hills westwards and ended at the lighthouse enclosure. The trees surrounding the lighthouse are still to be seen, as also is a portion of the old brick-built cart house.

The land side of the railway comprised the five houses in Alt Road "Clynder", "Altmouth", "Harefield", "Cross House" and Gaffney's shop. I well remember the owner, Mr Gaffney senior, as my pals and I had frequent encounters with him and his walking stick. We had a great passion for sitting on the wall and banging our heels on the Fry's Chocolate advert. The only other houses on this side of the railway were Lizzie Seddon's cottage, the original village pub, which stood where Manweb's transformer behind the signal box now stands, and the Station Farm (now demolished because of lack of drainage, approximately 1925). It was situated at the back of our only telephone kiosk at the junction of Sandy Lane with Alt Road. Alt Road was the only paved road, for Sandy Lane lived up to its name and was just a cart track through the sand. St. George's Road was non-existent and was part of a field, as were Windermere and Thirlmere Roads. There were two cottages in Sandy Lane; one, "Rose Cottage", still in existence, and another similar further down the lane and now the site of the pair of semi-detached bungalows adjacent to "Grey House". Between Frith's Ham Gate Farm and Pope's White Edge Farm, just on the bend in Alt Road, stood "Hawthorne Cottage" which was a tied cottage attached to White Edge Farm and occupied by one or other of the farm teamsmen. It was demolished about 1920.

In 1901, after the Boer War, changes began to take place. The first development started when the L. & Y. Railway started to take away the sandhills adjacent to School Road and Rathbone

4. Farm Dairy, Sandy Lane
Undated. The presbytery of Our Lady of Victories is to the right; the church itself is on the opposite side of the road. Colonel J. Graeme Bryson, a distinguished local resident, lives at "Sunwards", to the left.

5. Pharmacy, School Road c. 1931/32
Isaac Edwards and, later, his daughter Mrs Dilys Owen (shown in the picture as a child) owned the chemist shop from 1929 until 1978. The building was a pharmacy even prior to Isaac Edwards' time; the 1929 street directory describes it as a chemist owned by Stanley Taylor, in 1924 a John Denham owned it and in the 1913 directory the chemist was G.H. Cole. The shop is now a hairdresser's.

Road and for this purpose constructed a siding from a little of the Formby side of the Southport platform and running through the extinct wooden telephone exchange - alongside the west side of School Road. As they cleared the sand away and it got too far for the men to throw the sand, they moved the metals over it to get into contact with the sand again. It must be remembered there were no mechanical shovels or machines of any sort, and all the sand was loaded by hand. Usually, they brought about 60 or 70 trucks and when loaded I believe they went to Pilkingtons at St. Helens to be used in their glass making. At that time there was no other market for this type of sand. Thus, the site of what are now Rathbone and School Roads and Lower Alt Road as far as "St. Stephen's Lodge" was levelled off ready for building. However, in 1904 came the Hydraulic Brick and Stone Co. and they took over the sand concession from the L. & Y. Railway and started to produce their sand lime silica bricks. Their factory was built in Sandy Lane, opposite the railway siding. The houses "Ingleside", "Sandhurst", "Grange", "Gwynfa" and the bungalow "Orotava" now occupy that site. Their bricks had to be handled very carefully and could not be thrown about so, in consequence, these extra costs of handling made them too costly. Their only sale of any size was to the new Liverpool Cotton Exchange where they can be seen to this day and they have weathered very well so far.

A subsidiary company - The Hightown Land Development Co. - was then formed and Windermere and Thirlmere Roads constructed, and plots let off to builders with a reservation clause in their agreements that all materials should be purchased through the parent company, i.e. the Hydraulic Brick and Stone Co. This would be about 1905 and was really the beginning of the development in the village, for Mr Gregg began to build Rathbone Road and Messrs Felton and Blackhurst commenced operations in Blundell Avenue and Blundell Road with a Mr Nicholas also operating with the three bungalows on the other side of the Avenue, adjacent to Blundell Road.

The latter end of 1906, through most of 1907 onwards to 1914 saw my father building School Road and Lower Alt Road, whilst Mr Gregg opened up St.George's Road. He also continued with his operations slowly through to the outbreak of hostilities in August 1914. Incidentally the three houses in Lower Alt Road on the left hand side - Numbers 11, 13 and 15 - were sold by my father: Number 11 at £400, Number 13 at £500 and Number 15 at £575. Messrs Felton and Blackhurst carried on until 1917 when they built the greengrocer's shop in Lower Alt Road and also the pair of semi-detached houses, now "St. Stephen's Lodge" and "St. Ives".

As the population increased, there was a call for a club and in approximately 1906/7 a number of young men formed a soccer team, and they hired a pitch from W. Rainford and Sons which was situated behind what is now Frith's Dutch Barn, where they played for a couple of seasons with the goal posts facing east and west towards St George's Road. The Rainfords decided to plough up this field so their pitch was transferred to what is now Elmcroft Lane. This was the beginning of the Hightown Club.

About 1908, Hightown organised its own Voluntary Fire Brigade of which my two brothers and myself were very active members. Details of its membership and activities I have dealt with in another chapter. It was also in 1908 that the footbridge over the railway was erected as a result of a jury's verdict on a soldier, Tom Minors, who was killed by an express train whilst crossing the line.

At this stage of the village development, I would point out that Mr Mellard Reade, the Blundell of Crosby Estates Surveyor, and Mr Francis Weld, their Solicitor, decided that because of the fear of inundation, it would be gross folly to develop nearer to the shore than the two older houses in Lower Alt Road, i.e. "Sunset Corner" (No. 15) and "Dale House" opposite. All Mr Reade's layout for the Thornbeck Avenue area was based on this theory, so much so that the wooden bungalows that most of the older residents remember well were allowed to be erected close to the shore because they were beyond the development area. The concession for these wooden bungalows was given on condition that the owners kept the shore hills fenced to keep trippers out, which allowed the vegetation to multiply and keep at bay the sand erosion during windy weather. This concession was a very wise move for it very soon allowed the hills in the vicinity of the houses to consolidate and we had no more trouble with blown sand until about 1966 when the new development started and the bungalows were demolished. However Mr Reade's and Mr Weld's successors, together with Crosby Corporation, have taken into their extended development area a lot of ground much nearer the river and the shore, which I still think is playing with fire. This part of the coast has once before been the victim of a tidal wave and our only protection has been the massive range of sandhills which, however, were carted away during the War (without supervision) for sand bag protection in our large cities. The Ministry of Housing Inquiry at Waterloo Town Hall in April 1967 agreed with our fears and no more building development is to be contemplated until coastal defence works are completed.

6. Sunday School Outing, c. 1927
The four ladies in hats at the top are Sunday School teachers: (left to right) Phyllis Brownskill, Dora Brown, Florence Tiffin and Stella Brown. The two children in the top row are Wilfred Cook and Betty Neale; middle row (left to right) Iris Whitaker, Sidney Hall, Betty Baybutt, Stella Wardle & Jim Baybutt. Alan Deane is front left, next to the four Metcalf boys, an unknown girl and Nancy Dawkins. Photo taken at Frith's Farm where Dr. Welch lived at the time.

1912 saw Mr Michael Riordan open up Blundell Road beyond Blundell Avenue and he extended his activities in the years following, up to his death in the early fifties.

In the pre-war period of 1906 to 1914, two very important assets to village life came into being. About 1906 St. Stephen's Mission Church started with services in private houses, to be followed by Our Lady of Victories Mission in 1914. Both of these missions made a big impact on the life of the village, so I have devoted several pages to a more detailed account of their early activities.

After the Armistice in 1918, our firm transferred its activities to Sandy Lane and the houses in Sandy Lane and Elmcroft Lane are the results of our labours in that area. With Mr Riordan's activities on one side of the railway, and ours on the other side of the railway, the village slowly grew in size; but in 1928 and onwards, the market for this large type of house declined, principally, I think, because of the shortage of domestic staff. Girls who used to live-in with a salary of 5/- per week and 'all found' (for that was about the rate paid about this period) started to fight shy of domestic service and found work in Liverpool factories. Quite a large number found much better employment, finances and recreation facilities with the football pools firms. So in 1932, we came back to the shore side of the railway and opened up Thornbeck Avenue and St. Stephen's Road areas.

We confined our efforts to a smaller type of house which the housewife could run on her own, and in this area, we continued up to 1939 and also after the War from 1946 onwards until the mass-produced bungalows of Mark Road came in 1959, and the later development of Riverside, North Dunes, etc., in 1966. As there was only Mr Riordan and ourselves interested in the building development in the period between the two Wars and up to 1959 progress was a bit slow, but most of our clients were well satisfied. However, not all of our clients were swans and an occasional ugly duckling turned up.

Before I close there were two further milestones in the story of our village which I must not forget to relate. The first was the inauguration of the Ex-Servicemen's Club, known later as the Village Club, with a pavilion and sports ground, now the home of the third and fourth cricket and hockey teams of the Hightown Club and situated in Sandy Lane opposite "Grey House". Mr Alf Connell at that time (1920) lived at "Ennerdale", St. George's Road and he generously secured the lease on the field, obtained a redundant army hut which he fitted out as a pavilion, laid out two soccer pitches, cricket square, bowling green and a couple of tennis courts at his own expense for the benefit of the village lads of military age who were fortunate enough to return. We were augmented with quite a few of the staff from the Truant School.

A very successful period developed with considerable social activities until we originals got a bit too long in the tooth (even for bowls) and so gave way to the younger generation. The new generation carried on until they in turn were drafted into the services in 1939. After the War there was a dearth of youngsters interested so, in the long run, the Hightown Club took over and, as I have mentioned above, it is at present the centre of the third and fourth team activities.

The other but lesser milestone was the opening of a second sand, lime, brick company on the site of what is now Hester Close, about 1930 which, up to the outbreak of War, levelled all the sandhills in the Mark Road and Hester Close areas and also the remainder of the hills adjoining St. Stephen's Church north boundary. They closed down on the outbreak of War and, of course, all our sandhills in Thornbeck Avenue and beyond were taken away during hostilities for the sand bag protection of our big cities. Mr Mellard Reade, the Blundell of Crosby's Surveyor, met with an accident and died in 1940 and, with conscription being in force, a successor of any standing could not be found; hence the sand was carted off without any supervision, which has now resulted in the large-scale filling up of the development area to bring it up to 26 feet O.D. as originally intended by Mr Reade in his proposed layout for the Thornbeck Avenue district.

CHAPTER TWO

Hightown Hotel

I can remember the hotel since 1897 for as a seven year old boy I reckon I was just about sitting up and taking notice of things. I have no direct proof of the building of the hotel, but I have always understood that it was built with the demolished materials from the Kirkdale Jail; and certainly during my visits to the hotel in the course of work there, there is ample evidence of second-hand materials - the stables and boundary wall are proof of this theory.

Kirkdale Jail is now the site of Kirkdale Recreation Ground adjoining Rumney Road, Garnett Avenue, Brook Street and Sessions Road.

The last two public hangings in the Jail were in 1884 when Mrs Higgins and Mrs Flanagan were hung for the murder of some of their families for insurance money; and shortly afterwards it was pulled down. I have always understood that a Mr Molyneux built the hotel as a residential venture and certainly with the activity on the Rifle Range, the Waterloo Cup and coursing, and Grand National clients, they were kept fully occupied - and, of course, the bowling green was kept in use every day, summer and winter, and did a very good business when other greens were closed. At the southerly end of the bowling green was the picnic house (still standing) where they catered for school treats, and the children could cross School Road to play on the huge sandhills.

On the 1891 Ordnance Survey sheet there are only the Truant School, the hotel, the pair of semi-detached Railway cottages in Lower Alt Road, and the two pairs of semis in School Road which were built as married quarters for the Truant School staff. The rest was was just huge sandhills except for the old mortuary in Lower Alt Road where the War Memorial now stands. Lower Alt Road at that time was just a cart track to the shore and the tide at times came up the cart track as far as the mortuary. On the land side of the railway are shown five houses, now Hightown Stores, "Cross House", "Harefield", "Altmouth" and "Clynder". On the latter's coach house is a sandstone dated 1888 (and is still to be seen). There is also shown Frith's original farm behind the telephone kiosk (since demolished) and also the original village inn which stood on the site of the present Manweb transformer behind the signal box. The old inn was pulled down about 1908 and its materials were used in the building of the bungalow nearest to the railway in Blundell Avenue.

Gaffney's Stores was established in 1892 and my surmise is that the first development of Hightown as shown on the 1891 Ordnance Survey started shortly after the hangings at Kirkdale in 1888 or thereabouts. No further development took place until 1904.

I was told that Mr Molyneux had the brewery in Crosby Village which stood at the back of the George Hotel, corner of Moor Lane. This is my surmise so far as I can relate of the original opening up of Hightown, backed up from what was told to me by some of the older residents

7. Hightown War Memorial, with sand dunes
This early photo shows the war memorial adjacent to sand dunes, before the construction of houses in Riverside, Westway and North Dunes.

8. Gaffney's Store in the snow
An undated, but early photo. Gaffney's was an institution in Hightown, originally established in 1892 by Mrs M.J. Gaffney. It was a well - equipped store in two sections; one sold bread, cakes & confectionery, the other was a general grocery with a large mahogany counter and three or four members of staff serving customers. On 30th April 1970 the family left for North Wales and the store was taken over by Mr and Mrs Hesk.

of bygone days and, of course, the Ordnance Survey. From 1897, however, I have personal contact with all the history of the hotel and Hightown up to date.

The first licencee I remember was Mr Duncan, and in the early months of the year he was very busy catering for the coursing, and there were several coursing meetings during the year when all accommodation was taken up and the loft above the stables in School Road was also fully occupied by greyhound cages. After the coursing came the racing clients from Aintree and horse-drawn coaches were engaged to take them to and from the Racecourse. Of course, there were also a few permanent residents who went into Liverpool to business and back in the evening.

Then about April came the summer camps on the Rifle Range and all accommodation was booked by the officers and their families. The rankers were under canvas at the Formby end of the Range behind the firing points and on their free times they patronised the hotel bar to a very great extent. This in turn brought complications, for the troops clashed with the Irish farm labourers who came to local farms in February and went home again in October after the potato harvest. Each farm had an Irishman's shanty which consisted of two rooms in a convenient loft or outhouse, one with a grate and the other rigged up with a bed on which they slept.

As one can imagine there was no love lost between the troops who were mostly the old Militia, consisting of bricklayers, plasterers and builders' labourers, ships' stokers and firemen, and the fighting between them got out of hand on numerous occasions; so much so that in the early 1900s the licencee had one of the cellars converted into a bar and this was used exclusively by the labourers. This measure brought a little peace between the two factions. About the same time the top bar was extended and also during this period the lower portion of what is now known as the Captain's Bridge was built facing the bowling green and used as a billiard room and equipped with two full-sized tables. This was very popular with the public at that time.

At the top end of Blundell Road was a Pigeon Shooting Club where on most Saturday afternoons shoots took place, with 400 to 500 pigeons shot from five traps. The Club pavilion was complete with bar and restaurant and both victuals and staff were supplied by the hotel. The site of the Pavilion would probably be on the site of the house "Glenisla", Blundell Road, and the five traps faced the railway. To safeguard the trains from stray bullets, a big hoarding was erected just inside the railway wall.

At the northerly end of this pigeon shooting field were two small plots where the hotel grew asparagus for their guests. On the other side of Blundell Road, which at that time was only a sandy track alongside the sandhills, they also had a clearing surrounded by the hills where they grew more asparagus and other vegetables and potatoes. The site of this clearing is now taken up by two pairs of semis "Eastwood" and "Torresholme", "Seamore" and "Pendle", and also the houses "Ballure", "Selcoth", "Hollis" and "Norwood". The trees on the boundary of "Norwood" formed the southerly boundary of this clearing and in the trees were a couple of wooden huts in which the tools were stored.

The hotel also kept a couple of cows and never less than six pigs, which were kept in styes close by the entrance to the yard in School Road opposite Rathbone Road. I should imagine with all these assets to draw upon, the hotel would be almost self-supporting.

It was also plain to be seen that the stables and coachhouse accommodation in the hotel grounds was not sufficient for its needs because a large open shed, which held approximately five or six broughams or cabs, together with two or three loose boxes, were constructed on a level portion of the sandhills now taken up by Rathbone Road and clearly to be identified on the 1891 Ordnance Survey and almost opposite the yard entrance in School Road.

These wooden structures were only done away with when Mr Gregg started to build the houses in Rathbone Road in 1905 or 1906 and were the homes of several of the cockle women who frequented Hightown in the early 1900s. Their mode of living was collecting cockles on the shore behind the Rifle Range and marketing them in the Crosby, Bootle and Liverpool districts. Cockle Lizzie, Old Bridget and Clara (I remember well all three) were of Irish descent and very quarrelsome they were with any strange cockle gatherers and, needless to say, scared the wits out of us youngsters.

9. Village Green, early 1930s
In the photo is Mrs Dilys Owen (née Edwards) as a child with a friend, Tony Bush.

After Mr Duncan came two or three licencees who only stayed for short periods until Mrs Berry took over in the early 1900s and she and her daughters, Miss Grace Dyson and Mrs Stedman held the licence for many years until Mr Rimmer Wright's day, and he was followed by Mrs Hesketh who held the licence until her death a couple of years ago.

The only addition of any note in the last few years has been the enlarging of the bar and the off-licence department at the corner of School Road, almost opposite this residence. Here I will be a little critical of the siting of the wine shop's two entrances which are on the corner. Consequently, cars park exactly on the corner during opening hours, which is a contravention of the Highway Code. Sooner or later there will be a serious accident, for car parking at this point reduces the carriageway to one track only. Already it has resulted in the uprooting of the privet hedge of the Village Green as cars and lorries cannot negotiate the corner without their back wheels pulling up the hedge. There is plenty of room for wine shop cars on the hotel car park.

I might add that on the occasion of the Waterloo Cup winner being housed at the hotel, it led to boisterous parties and free beer for all patrons.

CHAPTER THREE

Truant School

My earliest recollections of the Hightown Truant School go back to the turn of the century when, as a young school boy attending a North Liverpool school, I heard from some of the boys who had had a spell in the school, of the strict discipline and loss of liberty enforced ruthlessly by the whole staff on the unfortunate kids. I must emphasise that these boys had not been before the magistrate and their only crime was playing truant. Needless to say, the stories got a little varnished at times but nevertheless, the threat of Hightown to all of us by any of the teachers was sufficient to quieten the most fractious of us and bring us to heel. It is all very well for our modern reformers to tell us that strict discipline is no deterrent to crime, but I can assure them that the threat of Hightown was one of the biggest aids our teachers had to keep order in the Liverpool schools of that period. It must not be forgotten either that the cane and strap were in general use not only by headmasters but by all teachers and used in plenty, and I agree I had a fair share of it. However, as previously mentioned, the threat of Hightown was viewed with horror and I don't think there is anybody of my age today who can remember any lad being sent to Hightown for a second spell - once being more than sufficient.

About 1898 a relative of our family came to live in one of the semi-detached houses that were originally built for married quarters, just opposite the school, and my brothers and I came for holidays for some years until we settled finally in the village about 1903 or 1904. From then onwards, I had a more intimate view of the school and its strict discipline (fortunately from the outside). I understand it was built for the Liverpool School Board by William Hall and Sons Ltd. of Christian Street, Liverpool, as were the two pairs of semi detached cottages opposite and I would surmise about the same time as the hotel and the five old houses in Alt Road, approximately 1880 to 1888. Incidentally, I recollect that William Hall and Sons were established in 1863 and their present activities are based at Grange Terrace, Wavertree. It was a very fine building, substantially built of brick and it seemed to me almost criminal when it was demolished. Surely some use could have been found for it for it was in excellent condition and would have made a very good hostel for University students or such-like. I expect the powers-that-be will call it progress but I and my generation wonder and suggest vandalism would be a better description.

The school was divided into two, the C. of E. section near to Blundell Road and the R.C. portion adjacent to the railway. At the period of my school days the Principal and Headmaster of the C. of E. side was Mr Leach and his deputy, Mr George, was in charge for Headmaster of the R.C. side. (I might mention here that Monsignor George, S.J., a notable figure in R.C. circles in the 1900s, was his eldest son.) A Mr Edwards used to be what we youngsters christened "The Catcher" for the C. of E.s, a Mr Callaghan for the R.C.s. They hunted the truants in their haunts and brought them out by train, and their term of discipline started for a period of more or less three months.

10. Hightown Truant School
Undated but the postmark on the reverse is 1912.

They wore a uniform of corduroy long trousers, jackets and waistcoat, with red socks and for footwear clogs reinforced with steel strips. When you realise that most of these truant boys were running around Liverpool in their bare feet at this period, the mere fact of enclosing their feet in these clogs was a hazard they found hard to bear. On Sundays and church holidays the C. of E. lads walked the 3½ miles to Great Altcar Church whilst the R.C.s ploughed their way along Sandy Lane, which lived up to its name and was just a track through the sand, to Little Crosby Church, also approximately 3½ miles, and of course, in full uniform and clogs. They did not exactly run or walk, but travelled at a light infantry gait all the way there and back, and woe betide any of them who spoke on the way, for they were caned for the least breach of discipline and in severe cases put into one of the cells which formed the northerly boundary of the building. There were, I should say, about 18 or 20 of these cells during its session as a truant school, and were extensively used for breach of regulations. These cells were about 10ft x 6ft with a window just below the ceiling and the doors were of 2" pitch pine with a small circular spy hole about 4½ft high with a flap cover over it for the teacher to see that all was well with the occupant. These cells were taken out after the Education Authorities took over the Liverpool School Board (I should think about the 1908/10 period). Several of the doors are still to be seen on the outhouses of "St. Stephen's Lodge", "St. Ives" and the greengrocer's shop in Lower Alt Road, which were completed approximately the latter end of 1914 or early 1915.

SCHOOL BOARD FOR LIVERPOOL.

The Truants' Industrial School, Hightown.

DIETARY.

Day.	Breakfast.*	Dinner.	Supper.*
SUNDAY	¾ Pint sweetened Coffee 6 to 8 oz. Bread with Dripping or Margarine	4 oz. Cooked Meat ½ lb. Potato, 4 oz. Bread *or* ¾ lb. Potato Green Vegetables	¾ Pint sweetened Tea 6 to 8 oz. Bread with Dripping *or* Margarine
MONDAY	1 Pint Thick Porridge ¼ Pint Milk 2 oz. Bread	12 oz. Suet Pudding (baked or boiled) with Treacle	Bread and Milk 8 oz. Bread ½ Pint Milk
TUESDAY	¾ Pint sweetened Cocoa 6 to 8 oz. Bread with Dripping or Margarine	4 oz. Haricot Beans 2 oz. Bacon ½ lb. Potato 2 oz. Bread	1 Pint thick Porridge ¼ Pint Milk 2 oz. Bread
WEDNESDAY	Bread and Milk (8 oz. Bread and ½ Pint Milk)	½ Pint of Cocoa or Soup 8 oz. Bread 2 oz. Cheese Lettuces or other greens	¾ Pint sweetened Tea 6 to 8 oz. Bread with Dripping
THURSDAY	¾ Pint sweetened Cocoa 6 to 8 oz. Bread with Dripping or Margarine	4 oz. Cooked Meat, with ½ lb. Potato & 4 oz. Bread *or* ¾ lb. Potato Green Vegetables	Bread and Milk 8 oz. Bread and ½ Pint Milk
FRIDAY	1 Pint Thick Porridge ¼ Pint Milk 2 oz. Bread	1 Pint Soup (with Peas, Barley, and Vegetables) 4 oz. Bread *or* Rice and Milk sweetened 3 oz. Rice ½ Pint Milk 4 oz. Bread *or* 8 oz. Fish and ½ lb. Potato	¾ Pint sweetened Tea 6 to 8 oz. Bread with Dripping *or* Margarine
SATURDAY	¾ Pint sweetened Cocoa 6 to 8 oz. Bread with Dripping or Margarine	Irish Stew and 2 oz. Bread	Bread and Milk 8 oz. Bread and ½ Pint Milk

* ¼ Pint of Milk to be added in all cases in Tea, Coffee or Cocoa.

In the Roman Catholic section one of the non-meat dinners may be given by order of Superintendent on their days of abstinence.

The school was pretty well self-supporting with the lads being supervised by senior staff, chief of whom was Mr Harry Absolam who was responsible for the maintenance of the boilers and general cleanliness of the premises. He was a colossal figure and ex-boatswain R.N. His voice could be heard all over Hightown as he put the lads through their paces.

At the southerly end of the enclosure were two wooden sheds and after big tides the lads collected hand-barrows out of these sheds, four to each barrow, and marched through the lighthouse grounds onto the shore, where they collected driftwood which had been washed up by the tide. This was taken to the two sheds, chopped and tied into bundles, and about every three months Frith's Farm sent a wagon and two horses, and they were loaded and taken round the various institutions in Liverpool. Most of the vegetables were grown either on the premises or on some ground adjacent to the school, where Blundell Avenue is now sited. Bread, meat and fish were collected by the boys from the railway station on a two steel-wheeled truck and we outsiders often gave the two lads a hand with the truck, to half carry and half wheel the foodstuff along the semi-paved footpath which in places had a foot or more of blown sand upon it.

11. View from Hightown Truant School
Undated. The photo shows the entrance to the school, with a view down School Road. The pair of semi-detached houses on the left were built for the staff of the school to live in, and are still standing.

The school was strictly for truants - juvenile delinquents were dealt with in other reformatories such as Holy Trinity at Grafton Street, and the old wooden two-decker Training Ships off Rock Ferry, i.e. the *Akbar* for C. of E. and the *Clarence* for R.C.s, the latter which was set on fire in the early 1900s by the lads and became a total loss. After the Education Authorities took over from the School Board the discipline relaxed considerably and parents were allowed to visit once a month; and so it carried on until August 1914, when everybody joined up, the staff included, and I think the school was pretty well closed until after Armistice Day.

I was away with all of military age from the village so what transpired during the four years of War I do not know, but there is no doubt that the most notorious period was during the headmastership of Messrs Leach and George in the late 1890s and early 1900s, under the jurisdiction of the Liverpool School Board and subject to the strictest discipline.

After the War, a Mr Graham became Headmaster and Principal in succession to Mr Leach and a Mr Pickering took over Mr George's duties, and a new staff, entirely all ex-service men, were installed.

Amongst the new staff were Walter Unsworth, Dick Haskayne, Bill Darwin and Alex Millar, all of whom became members of the Ex-Servicemen's Village Club, organised and financed by Mr Alf Connell who provided the field (on lease of course from the Blundell of Crosby Estates), a pavilion, bowling green, two tennis courts, two football pitches and a laid-out cricket square between the two soccer pitches.

With several alterations as to its objectives such as a remand home, for backward children, etc., etc., it carried on under successive headmasters, two of whom I call to mind - Mr Beswetharick and Mr Lock, but mostly the same staff until I should say 1936 or 1937 when the whole establishment was transferred to Penketh, near Warrington. After laying idle for a short period it was opened up again with a new staff under the headmastership of Mr Watson who was followed later by Mr Karen until about 1962 or 1963 when it was finally closed and the school transferred to North Wales at Port Dinorwic. Shortly afterwards, it was demolished and the site cleared for redevelopment.

CHAPTER FOUR
Voluntary Fire Brigade

Hightown began to expand shortly after the erection of the Hydraulic Brick and Stone Co.'s brickwork factory in Sandy Lane on the site of what is now occupied by the houses "Ingleside", "Sandhurst", "Grange", "Gwynfa" and "Oratava".

A subsidiary company, the Hightown Land Development Company, laid out Thirlmere, Windermere and Grasmere Roads and the other builders built a few houses in St. George's Road and Rathbone Road. School Road and Blundell Avenue followed shortly afterwards.

These houses were soon occupied and so the question of fire arose, for we were dependent entirely on Great Crosby Urban District Council's Voluntary Fire Service. They were horse-drawn and took considerable time to arrive here and consequently in approximately 1906 or thereabouts a Committee was set up and amongst the leaders were - Dr Matthews of "Lanefoot", Mr Tom Russell of "Cross House", Mr F.D. Graham of "Altmouth", Mr T. Pennington of "Clynder", Mr P. Campbell of "The Croft", Mr Sutton Pearson of "The Dunes" and Mr P. Reader of "Eastwood". With the co-operation of our local Little Crosby U.D.C., the Liverpool Salvage Fire Association were also asked for advice, and this was freely given. Their representative suggested a first aid hose reel with extension ladder and all tools, enclosed in a small van with the huge ladder housed on top of the van; and of course it was hand-propelled and relied on main pressure from the hydrant. The ladder was very heavy and required a good deal of handling for it was purposely made to reach the attic window at the hotel, Truant School, "Altmouth" and "Clynder" all of which were three storey buildings.

Liverpool Corporation at that period were centralising their fire appliances and concentrating on their horse-drawn fire engines; consequently, there were a number of these emergency hose reels redundant and a voluntary subscription in the village provided the money for its purchase.

Mr W. Gaffney provided a site alongside his shop for the erection of its housing, and the Little Crosby U.D.C. paid for the supplying and erection of the wooden station which incidentally, I remember cost £9.10.0 and is still standing and used as a store by Miss Gaffney.

The equipment consisted of a standpipe for the hydrant, keys and bar for turning on the water, 6 lengths of hose coupled together on a drum ready for running out, axes, helmets, hack saws, four sets of spare hose, and a 40ft length of 1½" or 2" high-pressure hose for use inside a building, and of course the extension ladder and a single ladder of approximately 20ft in length which was housed on top of the van.

This is the point where we youngsters came in and I reckon I was one of the youngest, being nearly seventeen years of age when we were asked to volunteer. It must be remembered that

12. Great Crosby Fire Brigade 1907
At that time the Crosby Brigade served Hightown. The crew is pictured in Coronation Road, Crosby, by College Road (Carnegie) Library; a pumping station now stands on the triangle of grass. The photo was taken from Alexandra Hall

13. Great Crosby Fire Brigade 1920
Taken at the fire station near Alexandra Park, Crosby: there is a social club on the site at present. Pictured is the brigade's first motorised engine, "The Buckley".

there were not many youths in the village at this period and at times the Hightown Club, which was only in its first year or so, had great difficulty in turning out a full team. We were organised into two teams, one being from those members whose occupation took them into Liverpool, and the other was made up from those who were in the village all day. We were trained by representatives of the Liverpool Salvage Association and soon got into the run of things - erection of standpipe, running out of the hose, breaking the hose at the nearest joint when enough hose had been run out, etc., etc., and then started the ladder drill. This was a tricky affair and fortunately in my days it never had to be used for any rescue work. It took four men to erect and the least slackness on any one of the four led to trouble. On two or three occasions Dr Matthews had to render first aid to members of the crew when the ladder got out of hand during erection or lowering, but no-one suffered any serious injury. Most of our ladder training was at the entrance to the hotel and we had to erect the ladders in readiness to rescue anyone out of the attic windows, over the front entrance.

Amongst our first volunteers were Herbert Hodgson, Will Gaffney, Jack Gaffney, Harry Russell, Atkin Marsh, Harold Marsh, Monty Yates, my brothers Jack and Jim and myself, Frank Blumer and Plummer Campbell.

Then came our first fire - about 1910 or 1911; this was at White Edge Farm's Dutch Barn. The blaze started in the afternoon and soon six bays of new hay and straw were ablaze. The barn was only 30 or 35ft. from the shippon and stable in which were tied up six horses and eight cows, and when we all rushed up with our van, the wall in front of the animals was already getting hot. Consequently, both horses and cows were leaning back at the full extent of their tethers and near panic as well.

The horses we soon got rid of, for one stroke of the axe on the halter rope and they were free, and dashed off to their pasture, which is now Elmcroft Lane.

The cows, being fastened with chains and leaning back were an awful problem until one of us thought of twisting their tails which resulted in them lunging forward and so we were able to unfasten the chain, and away they went after the horses. Then we concentrated on cooling the stable and shippon walls and so prevented them catching fire. Of course, all this took the best part of an hour and then came a clanging of bells and up rolled the Liverpool Salvage horse-drawn from Sandhills, followed shortly afterwards by Crosby Volunteers' Fire Brigade, also horse-drawn. The Salvage Officer wanted to know where the animals were and complimented us on saving the cows, which in all this type of fire are a menace to rescue because of their steel chain tethers.

He told Crosby Fire Brigade their services were not required, and then sent six of us home to get some sleep and to come at 10.00pm to relieve those still on duty. From then on we had to stand by and let the barn burn itself out, and just be on guard to see none of the sparks started a fire in the stables and shippon. We finally came away at about 8 o'clock on the Saturday evening, having been first called out on Friday afternoon at about 3 o'clock.

I would say that this fire was our first major effort and with an occasional turn out, mostly for fires in birds' nests under the eaves or gables, August 1914 arrived and we youngsters were otherwise engaged for a few years.

I understand that Frith's farmhouse thatch roof caught fire during this period and also the house "Abbotsmead" in St. George's Road was gutted, for that was one of the first jobs I had to do when I came home early in 1918 - restoring the whole structure.

In 1920 the local gas plant, which was on the site of "Ingleside", Sandy Lane, blew up smashing the windows of "Wayside" and "Kingsdale" which were newly erected. It was a corrugated iron building, wood lined, and over the years had been used as a petrol air gas plant, and there were three or four hundred 2-gallon empty petrol cans stored on one side. It had recently been turned over to hydrocarbon and there was a 600-gallon tank of hydrocarbon in a brick well outside. We cut the feed pipe off and sealed it and then filled the brick well with water and then tackled the blaze. The wood lining burnt furiously and the petrol tin stoppers were blowing off and exploding. Two or three of us got hit with them and had big bruises for some time afterwards.

14. Hightown Stores (formerly known as Gaffney's) 1992
The space to the right of the photo is where the Voluntary Fire Brigade kept their vehicle. The shop has now become a doctors' surgery.

The fire started about 6.00pm and we had to evacuate the two houses, "Wayside" and "Kingsdale" but towards midnight we had made things safe and my elder brother, who lived at "Wayside" was able to take his wife and children home again, as did Mr Dickman at "Kingsdale".

From then until Crosby Urban District Council took over from Little Crosby U.D.C. things were more or less quiet and the new Council co-opted two of our locals - Joe Baybutt and Stanley Crompton into the Crosby Fire Brigade, and these two members looked after the van and equipment up to and throughout the War period until finally taken over by the Lancashire County Fire Service.

That is the history of the Hightown Volunteer Fire Brigade as I remember it, and it must be noted that it was intended only as a first aid measure from the very beginning and to my way of thinking a well thought out proposition. It provided us with a good bit of excitement at times which we thoroughly enjoyed although resulting in us finishing up soaked to the skin, as everyone else who came within range of the hose, just before we shut off the hydrant after all chances of a flare up were over.

We must realise that at that period it was all horse-drawn traffic and not much of it either for everything went by rail, and I think it would be a very fair estimate to say that it would take anything from one to two hours to get assistance from Crosby, which again was at that time only voluntary with no stand-by crews at hand.

CHAPTER FIVE

St. Stephen's Church

I surmise that the date when Hightown began to expand would be approximately 1904 with the arrival of the Hydraulic Brick and Stone Company whose works were opposite the railway siding in Sandy Lane. The advent of this and their subsidiary company and the subsequent development of the area meant that the population grew during this two year period 1904 to 1906. Then came the call of our leading residents for something to be done about a Mission Church, thus St. Stephen's came into being.

The village for its size had a goodly proportion of public spirited residents who gave the matter great consideration and here I will mention a few of them. Mr P. Reader, "Eastwood", Blundell Road; Dr Matthews, Alt Road; Mr T. Russell, "Cross House"; Mr Graham, "Altmouth", Alt Road; Mr A. Marsh, "Glen Allan", Alt Road; Mr Sutton Pearson, Alt Road; Mr G. P. Campbell, "The Croft", Thirlmere Road; and Mr R. Radcliffe, "Westwood", Windermere Road; and quite a number of others who were quite willing to assist.

Being in the Parish of Sefton, contact was made with Canon Wells, and he in turn deputed the Rev. M. Lynton Smith of St. Nicholas' Church, Blundellsands, the big task of getting things organised and how well he fulfilled this task; either he or his curate attended the morning services which were held in the lounges in the above-mentioned leading residents' houses, for several years. As the number of worshippers increased, accommodating them all became a bit of a problem, and as Mr R. Radcliffe's house, "Westwood", had the largest lounge, his house became the favourite for the services. When even this became congested permission was obtained to use one of the truant school classrooms.

15. St. Stephen's Church
In this undated photo, the church is still surrounded by rough ground

In the meantime, a Committee was set up and eventually a site was obtained and plans for the Mission Hall and Church were put in hand. The site was originally surrounded by sandhills. Of course, the start of excavations for foundations, etc., brought hosts of sightseers whose children played on the slopes of these hills, destroying the starr grass, and in no time the whole area was a mass of shifting sand whirling around the building in course of erection, causing endless unnecessary trouble to all concerned. This sand erosion was to be a very costly item and was not finally curbed until about 1930, or thereabouts, when Messrs Sherstone and Owen of the Southport Sand Company eventually were able to remove the huge sandhill between the District Bank and the Church, and which is now the site of the new bridge over the railway, and also another huge sandhill close to the easterly side of the Church. Both of these hills were originally higher than the top of St. Stephen's roof and to give an idea of this sand menace, the Church was only completed at the latter end of 1914, but in 1921 our firm had to take off the east side of the chancel roof, the whole of the kitchen roof and the full length of the Church itself on the east side, for about 7 or 8 feet up. Where it was joined up can easily be picked out even now, for the row of copper clips holding the last course of new slates, which joined up with the original, are quite visible to this day. All the timber was rotten, slates and gutters together with the ceilings of the kitchen had fallen in and the whole lot had to be replaced. St. Stephen's was not the only sufferer from this sand erosion menace for almost all the houses on the west side of the school and Blundell Road had similar trouble to contend with. To anchor the sand was a problem not easy to accomplish for when planted with starr-grass the activities of local and tripper children playing on the slopes ruined all chances of the starr-grass getting established.

Eventually the U.D.C. had the contents of the bins and household rubbish tipped in the bottom of the hollows and the paper, etc., set on fire, then the residue sowed with hayseed and covered with sand; in no time there was a heavy growth of vegetation which arrested the wind erosion. However, I think the real success of this experiment was that the tippings gave off not a pleasant aroma, so the hollow was shunned by all, thus allowing the vegetation to get well established and undisturbed.

This in turn brought loud outcries and protests from the parents of the children and visitors about there being nowhere for the children to play, etc., etc., but as each hollow adjacent to the houses was so treated, their activities moved away from the houses to nearer the shore. Thus the vegetation was allowed to recover and the sand erosion overcome.

Getting back to St. Stephen's, I am afraid that all of us of military age were in the Forces when the new hall was opened and the sanctuary dedicated, thus there is a break in my St. Stephen's memories until late 1918 and during most of Rev. A. P. Millar's curacy. However, after the Armistice of 11th November 1918, and a little later the advent of the Rev. J. T. Davies' curacy, a more active use was made of the Mission Hall, whist drives and dances, etc., on week-nights and Saturday evenings, when the sanctuary was screened off, and for Sunday, the screens wound up ready for morning service. After a short period, Mr Davies said he did not like this

16. The Bishop of Warrington's visit to St. Stephen's Church

The Bishop of Warrington, Rt. Rev. Laurence Brown, dedicated the new porch at St. Stephen's Church on 5th October 1969. The Priest-in-Charge was Rev. John Todd (who became the first Vicar in 1971). Jim Savin, sidesman, is on the far right of the picture.

17. Pantomime Group, 1920s

The clergyman is Parson Hall from St.Stephen's Church. Below Parson Hall is Ruth Beswetherick who nursed King George V during his last illness. Ruth was born in Hightown and attended Waterloo Park School and Knaresborough Grammar School, before under undertaking nursing training at Westminster Hospital. Her father was the headmaster at the Truant School. Audrey Ruth (later Winter) is pictured, first left, bottom row.

arrangement and called for a separate building for whist drives and dances, reserving the hall for church services only. He asked me to accompany him to look at a war-time Y.M.C.A. hut which was originally sited at Sniggery Farm for the benefit of the S.W. Borderers. It had been pulled down and stored in a yard in Great Crosshall Street,Liverpool. So much of it had been taken away that it was impossible to do anything with it but, on our way home, passing through Litherland towards Ford, we saw some old Army huts being demolished and, on enquiring, were able to purchase one of them for £1 per foot in length at a cost of £70.0.0. This new addition satisfied Mr Davies and did yeoman service until it was sold to make way for the present Church Hall, approximately 1955 or 1956.

Its two main faults were - first it was a little bit too narrow and secondly it soon lost its heat due to lack of insulation when the fires went out. In approximately 1923-1924 "St. Stephen's Lodge", which was then known as the "Anchorage", was for sale. Mr Barnes and Mr Herbert were in office then and they asked me to contact Mr Bob Blackhurst, the owner of the property, which I did, and the house was bought. I think it changed hands at approximately £900. The Rev. F.E. Cooke took up residence when he married shortly after he took over the curacy, and it has been the centre of St.Stephen's activities ever since.

The pathway to both the Church and the new hut was very rough, being often piled up with drifting sand until 1930 when, as previously mentioned, Messrs Sherstone and Owen got rid of the big sandhill between the Church and the District Bank. To reach the hill on the east side of St.Stephen's they had to lay a sleeper track alongside the hut and around the church porch up to the hill, for it was carted to the railway by horse traffic only. This sleeper track was the best pathway that St.Stephen's had ever had. By 1932 Sherstone and Owen had finished and had left the track for use of the Church. It was getting into a bad state of repair and the Rev. W.R.H. Hall was able to purchase from the brick company, whose factory was on what is now Hester Close, all the throw-outs which could not be used for building. Then he called for volunteers to help lay them in lieu of the sleepers which had done such good service in the past. There was no lack of help forthcoming, with the ladies providing the refreshments whilst the work progressed.

For a start we concentrated on a portion alongside the hut and we made it approximately 9 feet wide, and two courses deep, the bottom course on the flat and the top course on edge. Alex Millar, the Manual Instructor from the Truant School and myself, being tradesmen, set out the levels and laid the bricks, ably assisted by Joe Baybutt and Billy Darwin, who brought squads of his truant school boys and supervised them carrying the bricks over the hills to the path.

The Verger, George Whittaker, was a great help with the levelling and spade work, and Mr Leslie Crane supplied us with half a dozen theatre spot lights for use when the nights closed in.

We started in late August 1932 and finished it at the end of November. A good account was given in the *Liverpool Echo* on 29th September 1932. It was a very successful venture which we all enjoyed. At the instigation of the Rev. W.R.H. Hall, Mr Millar and I made a commemorative slab in cement giving the date.

Later on, cars and waggons began to use the path and as the foundations were not made for vehicular traffic, two deep ruts soon formed, which held pools of water and eventually it had to be covered with asphalt, and the commemorative slab as well.

With the completion of this path and the starr-grassing of the vicarage and church sites, the whole area began to take on a more refined look and not so much a building situated in a wilderness. However, I do not think any of the original parishioners could have visualised the difficulties that had to be faced and overcome. My only regret is that succeeding committees could not see their way clear to follow the lay-out scheme originally intended by the first Committee of building the church in the east-west position, and converting the present building into what was intended it should be, i.e. the Village Hall.

Finally, no words can be too strong for the praise and endeavour shown by that first Committee and its stalwart Chairman - Rev. M. Lynton Smith of St. Nicholas' Church, Blundellsands, who was the leader and prime organiser in St. Stephen's infancy from 1904 - 1914.

CHAPTER SIX

Our Lady of Victories R.C. Church

The nearest R.C. Church to Hightown in 1904 when development had started, was St. Mary's, Little Crosby, and the village was part of Little Crosby Parish. The original population consisting mainly of farmers and their labouring staff were of that faith, and thought nothing of the three miles' walk to Little Crosby for Mass and likewise their children had this walk every morning and evening to the school.

The absence of church and school had a detrimental effect on any newcomers and it was not until I should think about 1914 that any action was taken for the founding of the Mission Church. It is to Messrs Gaffney and C. Russell that the credit must be given for these two stalwarts interviewed Father Gardiner at Our Lady's, Formby, and he promised them every help and suggested that if they could obtain the use of a suitable and acceptable room he would see that he or one of his curates would say Mass on Sunday mornings for them. Thus a start was made, and Messrs Gaffney and Russell were able to obtain the use of Mr Gregg's workshop at the back of "Claremont", St. George's Road, where he lived at that time. Their stay there was very short for they soon transfered to his new workshop and electric supply building at the top of St.George's Road, close to the water course and adjacent to the Blundell Estates' pump house. The workshop has since been demolished but the pump house is still in existence and forms part of P. Adams' small-holding. There they carried on with the Sunday services until the Mission Church was built and ready for use.

During all this period, whist drives were held every week in Gaffney's billiard room at the bottom of their garden and, with other activities, sufficient funds were accumulated to enable a site to be obtained and plans submitted for the present building to be erected. The site was at that time part of Lizzie Seddon's small-holding and consisted of a wooden stable and cart-house which had to be cleared and - here - I must depend on the only three left of the original workers - Mrs Gaffney, Mrs Berry and Mrs Unsworth, for in this period when the building took place, we of military age were otherwise engaged! From them, I gather that the building was completed by Mr M. Riordan in 1916, opened 7th May 1916, and the chancel consecrated but still administered by Father Gardiner and his curates from Formby Parish. It was intended as the Parish Hall and was so constructed that it could be converted for that purpose.

I understand that a site for the parent church was obtained close to the junction of School and Blundell Roads. However, in 1925, Frith's Station Farm was condemned and demolished and the site cleared because of lack of drainage. The plot in Blundell Road was given up and the site of the farm to the rear of our only 'phone kiosk was obtained and still is the prospective site for the parent church. Shortly before the transfer to the farm site, approximately 1924, plans were approved for the presbytery on a portion of the farm plot facing Sandy Lane and on completion Father Horrabin was appointed and Father Gardiner handed the

18. Our Lady of Victories Church, interior
An undated, but early photo.

19. Archbishop Beck's visit to Our Lady of Victories, June 1968
Archbishop Beck is pictured leaving the presbytery of Our Lady of Victories, watched by a guard of honour, for a confirmation ceremony in the church. Nine girls and eleven boys were confirmed during the service. Canon Francis Danher, the Parish Priest of Our Lady of Victories, accompanied the Archbishop.

administration over to Father Horrabin, and it has been run as a separate parish ever since.

*20. **Altcar Grange.***
An undated photo

However, each priest has had the combined job of looking after his parish and having certain duties connected with the R.C. Educational Authorities in Liverpool.

Father Fox followed Father Horrabin after the First World War and in the years afterwards up to 1956 or 1957 several other priests were in charge. However, about the above date, Father Kieran was in charge and it was he who was responsible for the inside alterations and the addition of the new entrance porch on the south elevation.

The Grange Farm on Altcar Rifle Range has quite a few connections with R.C. history of the Reformation period and the old brick barn still in existence was once used as the Church. Here there is, I understand, a divided opinion amongst historians as to whether Grange Farm was a monastery in its own right or a granary attached to Stanelaw Abbey. One thing certain is that it was in the occupation of the monks at the time of the Reformation and most of the priests who escaped Cromwell's troops and got away to Ireland, passed through Grange Farm on the way to the boats.

From time to time various religious relics have been found in the old barn and Mr Jack Hesketh who was the tenant farmer under Lord Sefton at the time the Mission was founded (1911 or 1912) presented Father Gardiner with a silver chalice which had been found in the Barn, for the benefit of the new Mission. I have not seen it personally, but I have a photograph which was given to me by Mr Bryson. My cousin, who has had considerable experience in church history as Deputy Chairman of Carlisle Antiquarian Society, tells me that he dates the chalice as post-Reformation.

Another interesting find from the barn was a sheet of metal found by Dave Bullen Snr. who worked for Mr Hesketh as a teamsman for some years. He lived at the pump cottage at the top of St. George's Road, and his family used this metal sheet for blowing up the fire in the kitchen grate (for they had neither gas nor electricity and were entirely dependent on the coal fire for cooking and hot water). I believe that on one of Father Gardiner's visits, this sheet was put up to boost the fire (no doubt to make a cup of tea) and some curious markings on it made him examine it more intently. When cleaned up a trifle, it turned out to be a bronze plaque with raised figures of the Last Supper. From my memory of it when I saw it being cleaned and painted by Fred Mella it was approximately 27 inches long and 15 inches wide. Fred Mella was an artist at his trade, i.e. painter, and had his quarters in what is now the hairdressers' in Lower Alt Road. It was there I saw the plaque when he was working on its restoration and from him I heard the story of where and how it had been discovered. Father Gardiner asked him to restore the plaque and also loaned him a canvas oil painting (depicting the same subject) as a guide for the colours.

Both the chalice and the plaque as far as I know are still at Our Lady's, Formby, and whilst Canon Danher has seen and obtained all details of the chalice, I do not know whether anyone else has a clue as to where or what has happened to what I would describe as 'Old Dave Bullen's Plaque'

This then is the story of Our Lady of Victories Mission Church from its beginning as I remember it and whilst the dates given are approximate, I do not think they are far from being correct.

CHAPTER SEVEN

Crosby Lighthouse

Crosby Lighthouse, as I remember it, was a square brick-built tower with house attached at the foot of the tower. It was a massive affair and had an iron verandah close to the top for observation purposes and the cleaning of the windows, and was whitewashed throughout, both tower and house. A few yards away was a small two-roomed cottage with a shed for a cart at one end. It was situated almost on the shore but in the middle of very high sandhills and about a quarter of a mile from Hightown Station. The remains of the building are there still to be seen.

There was only a cart track through the sandhills and part of this track is still to be observed as it now forms part of a garage approach to the house "Lyndhurst" in Blundell Road, Hightown.

In 1897-1898 no vehicle could get any further than the railway crossing, and that is as far as the Crosby fire engine was able to reach when the disastrous fire occurred at the lighthouse, which as far as I can recollect was early 1898. There were four people and a large collie dog lost their lives in the blaze. These persons included a Mr Buckley who was in charge of the lighthouse, his wife and a lady visitor.

21. Crosby Lighthouse (drawing)
Undated

The lighthouse was never restored but later on in that year, Holy Trinity Industrial School Governors took a lease on the holding and built on to the southerly side of the house a brick dormitory and for years afterwards the boys from the school in Grafton Street spent their summer holidays in the enclosure, the older boys in tents, and the younger ones in the dormitory. Dr Noel Chavasse, who won the double V.C. award in the 1914-1918 war, spent the whole camp period with them and we locals used to have quite a few cricket matches with them on a field adjoining the railway which was used for pigeon shoots.

22. P.C. Bond
Joseph Bond, the hero of the Crosby Lighthouse fire.

Before the boys' camping holiday started, the girls' contingent of Holy Trinity School, in Nile Street, spent their holidays also in the enclosure, and there were also other similar schools who had their summer recess in the enclosure.

When their lease was finished, the landowners allowed a Boy Scout Association from Waterloo to use the site and this brought us almost to the outbreak of war in 1939.

In one of Jerry's many bombing attempts on Fort Crosby in 1941, a large bomb dropped almost on the back doorstep of the house and only for the fact that the walls were 2ft. 3ins. thick, there would have been some casualties, for there were in addition to the tenants - Jack Makin and his wife - about fourteen or fifteen people who had come from Liverpool to escape the bombing, and I had the job of condemning the house as unfit.

Later on when building materials were in so short supply, we took off the slates and all the usable timber, and on the underside of one of the bedroom flooring boards in blue pencil was written "This floor was laid by Thomas Goulbourne of Formby Street, Formby. Nov : 1898".

CHAPTER EIGHT

Hightown Club

My earliest recollections of the Hightown Club go back to the year 1906 when, as soon as Mr Gregg had finished the south side of Rathbone Road six or seven young men took on the tenancy of No. 9 and called it "Ye Shanty".

As far as I can remember, they included Messrs M. S. Yates, R. Lees, F. Blumer, H. Marsh, P. Lancaster, A.D. Derviche Jones and H. Turner. They all lived at "Ye Shanty" and were looked after by a lady housekeeper, whose name I think was Miss Humphries. Assisted by H. Russell Jnr., J. Gaffney, E.S. Dorning and several others, these youths were the founder player members of the Hightown Club when they started their soccer team.

Incidentally, quite a number of them were also connected with the Blundellsands Amateur Dramatic Society and R. Lees, F. Blumer, Monty Yates and A.D. Derviche Jones had leading parts in quite a number of their plays prior to and after the 1914-18 war.

23. Sandy Lane

"Ingleside" was the home of the late Lieutenant-Colonel Michael Cook and his brother Dr W.H.R. Cook, who predeceased him, both well known residents of Hightown

They rented from W. Rainford Senr., of White Edge Farm, in the autumn of 1906, the field behind what is now Frith's Farm and the pitch ran east and west, the easterly goal posts being the present Dutch Barn and the westerly posts towards the back gardens of St. George's Road houses. After one season there, W. Rainford ploughed this field for a root crop and transferred them to the Yeomanry field off Sandy Lane, which had recently come under his tenancy after the Yeomanry had vacated Hightown. This new pitch faced north and south and the northerly set of posts would be sited approximately in what is now Mr Winter's back garden in Sandy Lane. They played on this pitch for another couple of seasons until the four sponsors mentioned in the *Crosby Herald* History of the Club (8th December, 1961) i.e. Messrs Campbell, Graham, Russell Senr., and Sutton Pearson, had arranged with Mr W. J. Blundell of Crosby Hall for a lease on the present ground, which was then under the tenancy of Mrs Ellen Frith of Station Farm (now demolished) and access to the ground was via the farm yard close to the telephone kiosk.

As soon as the lease was completed the Sergeants' and Officers' Mess Huts left by the Yeomanry were obtained and moved across Sandy Lane to their present site of the old pavilion, one at each end for dressing rooms and the portion between them was enclosed to form the general room surmounted by the clock and its pediment.

24. Hightown Club, tennis courts

An undated view. The Hightown Open Junior Lawn Tennis Tournament was held annually. The Crosby Herald *for 11th August 1978 described the tournament as "the largest junior tennis tournament in the country". Stoniers, the Liverpool china retailers, at some time sponsored the tournament, which eventually discontinued in the early 1980s*

For the first couple of seasons, when short of players, local youths often helped out and Jack Bullen of Moss Farm, Herbert Hodgson, the local plumber, Jack Caley, the chemist, my elder brother Jack and myself all had very good games helping out when the necessity arose.

As for the rest of the Club history, I am certain that at the time when Mr A. H. Connell formed the Village Club he also had the three grass tennis courts laid out, adjoining Sandy Lane, and made a present of them to the Club.

Finally, I would like to add that Monty Yates and Francis Blumer were very active members from the Club's inauguration until a few years ago, and played a major part in the Club's management and activities throughout the whole of the life of the Club.

CHAPTER NINE

Land Drainage

The question of land drainage in S.W. Lancashire coastal areas has always created a number of problems and various schemes have been brought forward from time to time in dealing with the situation. The present huge pumping station close to the River Alt floodgates which is costing thousands of pounds is part of a scheme to rid these areas of the surplus water content in the ground. However, the following comments only concern the difficulties in our village and its immediate vicinities.

It must be remembered that underneath the present village lies the remains of an old forest with a peat bed of various thicknesses, which during the course of time has been covered with an accumulation of blown sand, and this has resulted in a layer on top of the peat of various depths. The School Road district has a depth of almost 12ft of sand whilst Blundell Road and towards Sniggery it is only about 3ft average and almost nil in the region of Sniggery. The same conditions apply on the shore where it is plain to see that the peat bed gets more exposed as one walks toward Hall Road. On the land side of the village the layer of sand on top of the peat is very thin and it is obvious that a lot of farm land in our area is a combination of the sand layer mixed with small peat which has been ploughed into it over the years, and it will grow almost anything, as can be seen by the crops now being harvested.

Hightown has been built to an average height of 26ft O.D. which is only 9½ft above a 31ft tide in Liverpool Bay. It is only a very small margin when one takes into consideration that a 6ft and over surge can occur with a W. or S.W. gale, as per Holdens and Lavers Tide Tables for Liverpool Bay. Consequently, our safeguard has been the massive sandhills which the new development is using in order to fill up to something near to 25 or 26ft O.D. From the Ordnance Map figures it will be noted that the natural fall in the contour of the ground is from the barrier sandhills which are the highest point in the area and falling gradually towards the Moss Lane and the Pheasant Inn. A comparison of this fall taken from Ordnance Survey sheets shows School Lane and Blundell Road to average 26ft O.D. whilst the Moss Lane and the Pheasant Inn are only 14ft O.D. and in certain readings as low as 13ft O.D. It will be seen from these figures that the natural flow of surplus water will follow the lay of the land and it is pretty evident that when moss land was first drained and made habitable the parties responsible took full advantage of this natural feature of the ground, hence the main water course was opened up along the Moss Lane and on towards the railway. There it was culverted under the railway and through the hills to the River Alt outlet where a valve was inserted which closed when the tide came in and prevented the tidal water from flooding the surrounding area.

Deep cross ditches were also constructed, most of them 4ft and 5ft deep and 5ft to 6ft in width, and in wet periods these water courses and cross ditches acted as a natural reservoir for they held a great amount of water at times of flood.

To these cross ditches were connected the farmers' land drains of 4" earthenware pipes with open joints laid in the ground and low enough so as not to interfere with the ploughing activities. The land drains are very important in all arable ground, more so even than manure and fertilisers, and are the main factor in keeping the soil from going sour and sodden.

It was a well thought out scheme in my opinion and was very satisfactory up to the early 1900s. Also the Blundell of Crosby Estates installed a pumping station at the top end of St. George's Road which forced the drainage water through the culvert and into the River Alt in the times of flood. However, when the houses started to be built and occupied (1905 onwards) there came the great question of the disposal of the household rubbish and I regret to relate the local council started to fill in these cross ditches with this household refuse and continued to do so until the amalgamation with Great Crosby U.D.C. in 1932. At a rough estimate I would say over 2,500 yards of cross ditches were filled up during this period. Of course, most of the ditches concerned had a 9" pipe laid in them before filling started but I suggest they are long since blocked up and not working. In 1969 the Crosby Corporation had to open up the ditch opposite "Rose Cottage" in Sandy Lane, and re-lay it because it was not working and interfered with the drainage at "Rose Cottage".

25. 'Near Altcar' by John Henry Williams.
View looking south-west amongst the sand-dunes at the mouth of the River Alt, across the Mersey to Wirral and the Welsh hills. Note the lighthouse in the centre background. Oil on canvas, 1856. Painting reproduced courtesy of National Museums, Liverpool (The Walker).

The natural reservoir contained in the wide and deep ditches was also destroyed for, when full in flood times, they held a vast amount of water. Consequently, the flood water could not get away in wet weather and the water level in the whole of our area rose considerably. This is easy to be seen in the lower-laying localities of Blundell Road, Sniggery, Elmcroft Lane and Windermere and Alt Road gardens. Not only has the water level in the ground risen but now that the pipes are blocked up the flow to the water course is greatly retarded and the water cannot get away as it should.

Up to 1914 the fields on the shore side of the railway towards Sniggery were well cultivated and there were at least three open ditches which ran in a N.E. direction from the sandhills, adjacent to Fort Crosby to the water course along Moss Lane, and thence to the outlet. They were open through the permanent way and encased one each side of the railway for the use of the troops, the R.G.A. at Fort Crosby, and the S.W.B. at Sniggery. No notice was taken of the land drainage and the ditches each side of the railway were filled up for the full width of these roads. Afterwards, as these ditches were not functioning, the railway filled up their portion through the permanent way and this is the position as it stands today - no outlet for the surface water from the shore side of the railway to the Moss Lane water course. I know of only one four-inch land drain between Sniggery and Grange Crossing at Altcar which is in working order.

26. Hightown Pumping Station

Situated in the grounds of Altcar Rifle Range, work started on the pumping station in 1968 and finished in 1972. Eventually costing £1.25m, it is the biggest of the eight pumping stations, draining 8,782 acres, along the 17 mile River Alt, which rises in Huyton. The pumping station replaced a set of traditional tidal gates that had been built in 1930, a time when many farmers and householders kept boats for the 'wet season'. The modern facility has 4 storm-weather, and 4 dry-weather pumps.

In the summer of 1969 the Club cleaned out one or two of the existing ditches surrounding the Rugby ground and the ditch between the old Village Club ground and Sandy Lane. The farmer has also cleaned out the extension of this ditch as far as the railway which should help considerably to get rid of the surplus water at flood times. However, these cleaned out ditches only deliver into other ditches which have been filled up and piped. In some cases a trickle manages to get through the pipe but mostly it is held up until it soaks away with consequent flooding of gardens to houses close by. I know of several houses where the foundations cannot help but be in the water at flood periods and I think everyone will agree this will not do the house or its occupants much good.

This then is the situation of the land drainage at present and no more ditches should be filled up or deteriorate for lack of cleaning out. My view has always been that our first drainers who rid the ground of its surplus water and made it ready for arable farming had remarkable and far-seeing insight into what was required and only opened up a ditch where it was necessary. To fill them in again is just asking for trouble and should not be allowed. The interference with the land drainage is the cause of most of the flooding of the new industrial and housing estates, for a nice dry well-drained area of arable land is taken over for development. Then trenches are excavated for sewers, water and gas mains, telephone and electric cables, and as the land drains are in most cases within 3ft of the surface, they are all wrecked completely. Added to this, the cross ditches are filled in and thus in no time the whole of the area is back to the state it was in originally before the farmer drained it: and we call it 'Progress'. I wonder!!

I have always understood the first drainers were called 'reamers', because they excavated to the ream in the ground. The 'ream' is the local term for that point in the ground on the water level, and just above the peat bed in most cases. Without special equipment and steel pilings and pumps, no further depth can be obtained and even then it is a very costly business. A lot of the extra costs on Kerslake Way were caused through this ream and the running mixture of sand and water which falls quicker than it can be excavated. This feature applied also to the excavating of the original ditches and I have seen quite recently some of the ditch sides fall in when the farmer has tried to clean them out a bit deeper.

Some historians are of the opinion that the reason for such a lot of families in the Southport and surrounding areas bearing the surname "Rimmer" is that they were descended from the original drainers - such as 'Jack the Reamer' - which name in the course of time has been slightly abbreviated to 'Jack Rimmer'.

CHAPTER TEN

River Alt & Coastal Areas

Seventy years ago I had my first view of the River Alt and the Hightown shore with an abundance of fish and a lovely stretch of clean sand all the way up to the south side of Fort Crosby. From there onwards towards Hall Road at various places the peat bed showed itself. It was always possible to see anglers with rod and line at various points on the river bank. I understand it was a common sight throughout its length until about 1896 when pollution first started. One of my earliest recollections of this trouble was in early 1897 when throughout that winter my father was engaged in rebuilding the flood gates bridge at Altcar Rifle Range. He brought me with him from Liverpool when the weather was good, and I remember seeing dozens and dozens of dead and dying fish held up at the back of the flood gates when the tide was in. His staff had a good deal of trouble getting rid of them when the gates opened as the tide went down. My father told me that it was due to the West Derby Sewage Farm of the Liverpool Corporation becoming overloaded, so the only alternative was to allow untreated sewage to pass into the river. He also told me that the River Alt Commission which administered the river at that period, served two or three injunctions against the Sewage Farm, but I am afraid it was the lesser of two evils, i.e. either to carry on with the pollution or proceed with a new larger sewage disposal works which they did. But until this was completed, the poisoning of fish continued.

However, up to the 1920s there were always eels to be obtained in the muddy stretch of the river from the flood gates to the Lower Alt Road area, and from there to the outlet flukes could be caught in the sandy stretch, but not with rod and line. The eels were prodded for with what is locally called a 'shar' which consists of a three-pronged fork about a foot long with saw-tooth edges and mounted on ten or twelve foot poles used from a boat drifted stern first with the current. You plunged the shar into the mud at the bottom of the river and the eels were trapped between the saw-toothed edges of the three prongs. For the flukes a 'prickle' was used and this consisted of about a dozen barbed steel pins six inches long, fitted into a cross piece of hardwood, and fitted to a ten or twelve foot pole and looked more like a vertical rake. This was also used from a boat and the prickle was plunged into the sandy bottom of the river, and the flukes were impaled through their backs as they lay on the sandy bottom.

My experience in this type of fishing was in the period 1900 to 1906 when I used to accompany either Fred Lindsay, who owned the river gig *Gleaner*, or his friend and partner Tom Leadbetter, better known as 'Shrimp', on their fishing expeditions. At weekends and subject to the tides we used to sail up to the flood gates where they adjourned to Bob Formby's at the canteen on the Rifle Range (now the Red Rose Club). We played about until they returned about 1½ hours after highwater and then we drifted downstream with the current with one of them prodding with the shar from the stern as we drifted slowly down towards Hightown. The other kept the boat in the middle of the stream taking advantage of the current. In a very short time the bottom of the boat was covered in a wriggling mass of slippery eels. On arriving opposite Lower Alt Road the boat was tied up and we parted, me to further games and Fred and Tom to another session, but this time at the hotel bar. The week of low tides we drifted down the river on the last of the ebb tide and as from the Lower Alt Road junction to Hall Road the river bottom became sandy, the prickle was substituted for the shar and so our efforts were concentrated on the flukes that frequented the sandy bottom of the river. Our drift with the ebb was timed so that we arrived at the river mouth just in time to meet the tidal wave of the incoming tide, which brought us back to Hightown without any effort on our part. The tidal wave or 'bore' rocked the boat a great deal and added to our enjoyment. Of course it is still to be seen as it surges up the river and climbs up the river banks two or three feet each side, and at heights of four to twelve inches across the stream above the ebb water. When it reaches the flood gates the extra pressure closes the gates, and then the water gradually backs up until high water after which it subsides until there is more pressure on the fresh water side of the gates, and they open again. As I have mentioned earlier, there were eels and flukes to be obtained with the shar and prickle up to 1920, but since then the pollution has increased very much and there is no life of any sort in the polluted waters.

27. Submerged Forest

These are the remains of a forest that is thought to have covered the Mersey basin; the forest extended from the Sefton Coast to the Wirral, connecting Lancashire to Cheshire. Tree trunks and peat can be seen off the coast of Hightown. Remains of the forest have also been found elsewhere, such as in Formby, Waterloo and Seaforth.

About 1930 the old Catchment Board's Engineer, a Mr Heaton, decided that the flood gates were holding up the flow of the river in flood periods and so those new sluices were built on the railway side of the flood gate bridge, and this scheme proved a huge success, for instead of the river being in flood for a week after a very wet spell, it was up and down in a night, and we found this out very quickly for it became impossible to row a boat against the current as formerly and we were forced to put a line on to any boat working against the current and tow the boat from the bank. Mr Heaton was of the opinion that the increased flow from the new sluices would scour the river bottom of the mud and, as well as increasing the flow, would lower the river bed, and he told Mr Mellard Reade and myself he would estimate that in a few years the channel would deepen approximately 7ft and this has been fulfilled. One result of this deepening has enabled the Drainage Board to construct a new culvert from the railway at the top of St. George's Road under the railway through the sandhills to the outlet on the river bank and much lower than the original stone culvert which was in a bad state of repair. The new culvert did away with the need for the pumping station that adjoined the railway and the pumps and gas plant were taken out, and the building now forms part of Mr R. Adams' smallholding. It has also enabled the Drainage Board to deepen the main water courses and this scheme was completed just before the War in 1939.

Up to 1918 there were no sandhills on the Rifle Range side of the river further than just north of the boat yard at the bottom of Lower Alt Road, and Formby shore continued right up to the point. For several years before and after the Boer War the Duke of Lancaster's Yeomanry held camp in Sandy Lane and their stables (eight or ten wooden structures) stood on the Rugby pitch opposite "Rose Cottage". To enable them to cross the river the Royal Engineers constructed a trestle bridge at the junction of Lower Alt Road with the river which enabled them (as soon as they passed over) to have an open shore with no hills near to interfere with their manoeuvres, and it was a grand sight for us youngsters to see them re-forming sections from four abreast to a doubledrawn outline and back again, and finally the charge of the whole regiment with the trumpets blaring forth which made the day for us.

Lower Alt Road being open to the shore and considerably lower, allowed the high tides to come up to the cart track which formed the road then. I have seen the tide almost at the end of School Road in a high tide with a gale behind it and, on several occasions, a number of pitch pine logs used in the launchings at Cammell Lairds were deposited by these tides close to the War Memorial. It must be remembered however, that the road had been filled up approximately six feet since those early days and the building up of sandhills on the Rifle Range side of the river has also helped to remove this menace.

Seeing how easy it was for the tide to almost reach the village, and in view of the fact that our village at the highest point is only 9½ feet above the highest tide in Liverpool Bay, influenced me very strongly in December 1963 to protest vigorously against any building schemes being contemplated until strong coastal protection schemes were completed. (The fears of inundation were fully justified at the Ministry of Housing Inquiry in April 1967, when the

Lancashire County Council and Ministry of Housing experts on coastal erosion agreed with my fears with the result that the findings at the Inquiry were that no more planning permission should be given until the shore had been fully protected from inundation.) Unfortunately, notwithstanding that the notices in the local press stated definitely that objections had to be sent to the Ministry not later than 23rd December 1963, (my objection went to the Ministry on 9th December) planning permission was granted for the twenty-eight acres (which were completed around 1969) on 17th December 1963. My view has always been that there is no appreciable difference in the contour of the land between Hall Road West and Lower Alt Road and all should have been subject to the Inquiry's findings. How one small acreage was given planning permission before objections had been fully scrutinized by the Ministry is beyond me entirely.

Another source of trouble with the meandering of the River Alt took place between 1920 and 1930 when the river extended its outlet towards the Gladstone Dock and created havoc with the houses on the west side of Burbo Bank Road, quite a number of them being undermined by the action of the tide and collapsing on to the shore. Old Shrimp, with whom I sailed in the boat, *Gleaner*, and several other longshoremen from Brighton-le-Sands told me that they always understood that at one time the Alt joined the Mersey in the Gladstone Dock area, and it would make its way back there again in due course. They assured me that several attempts had been made over the years to try and curtail it, but it had always broken through the barriers and made its way in a southerly direction again. There was, until about six or seven years ago, evidence of a diversion attempt just opposite the new pumping station on Riverside where across the river and carried up both banks, were the remains of an old brick causeway about ten feet wide; and we often used to wade across it when we went bathing or cockle gathering on Formby Shore. When the diversion attempt was made I do not know, for all my enquiries over the years have drawn a blank and Jack Young the Alt Bailiff, who was in charge of all river works from 1896 to the early 1900s could find no records either.

28. Coastal erosion
Taken at The Serpentine, Blundellsands in the late 1920s, the photo shows the damage wrought by the River Alt as it made its way to the sea.

Mr Young's theory for the tendency of the Alt to encroach into the sandhills was due to the loose sand being blown by the prevailing wind along Formby shore and into the river's right (or seaward) bank and consolidating there. This naturally made the right bank much harder than the left bank so all the eroding and alterations to bends over the years have taken place on the left bank. To prevent the accumulation of the blown sand adjacent to the river Mr Young and his men built a series of thorn groins on the Formby shore a few hundred yards from the river bank. Throughout his term of office they were kept in strict repair. In the week of low tides they effectively arrested the blown loose sand and, when the high tides came the week after, it was all washed away even at times leaving a depression at the base of the groins which soon filled up the next week of low tides. His successor Charlie Shaw did not maintain these groins after approximately 1910 or 1912 and, since then, the large sandhills have arisen on the right bank of the river; and moreover the bend that originally turned west at the bottom of Lower Alt Road has been pushed approximately 500 or 600 yards further south and necessitated a big reinforcing project and revetment to the left bank, I would think about 1932 or thereabouts.

Another, and almost successful, attempt at diverting the course of the river was made in 1929 when a new channel was blasted with explosives at the southerly end of Fort Crosby. It was organised on a voluntary basis and public subscription with Mr Mellard Reade at the head and I volunteered to assist. There was a series of six explosions and the new scheme was to have the river following the explosions along the new cutting. I have a series of nine photographs that I took during operations and they have kept very well over the years. Every 10 feet we sank a tube with 7lbs of gelignite 9ft down for, I think, 80 yards in length. They were connected with their fuses to the battery and so exploded. The first explosion was a huge success and the river surged up the new cutting like a mill race. When it hit the end of what had been exploded it crashed over and soaked every one of us, but as it was very hot weather nobody came to any harm. However, the second blast went wrong as we came upon a former bed of the river and, instead of sand for the 9ft down, we had 6ft of sand and 3ft of mud. Consequently, our pumps could not blow the mud away and the explosives could get no further than the 6ft of sand. The exploding of the second blast was the cause of the failure and Mr Reade wanted to dig out the mud at 10ft intervals and put in more charges. However, he was outvoted and we proceeded with the other four blasts without any trouble. When completed I am sorry to report that the incoming tide came up the old channel approximately one and half minutes before it came through our new channel. The whole scheme depended on the scouring and consolidating of the new channel by the currents of both incoming and outgoing tides. I am afraid that the existing channel, having the priority by one and a half minutes, resulted in the failure of the whole scheme. There is no doubt in my mind that if Mr Reade had not been outvoted over the second blast and had been allowed to carry out the original scheme of having the river follow our explosions, all would have gone according to plan and the old channel would have filled up. After a fortnight with two lots of tides you could hardly see where we had operated, for the new channel was totally obliterated. Mr Reade was very upset over our failure but I am afraid it was another case of too many cooks giving their opinions as in the case with many voluntary schemes such as this.

GREAT CROSBY URBAN DISTRICT COUNCIL.

Proposed diversion of the River Alt through the Sandbank by blasting a new channel.

OUTLINE OF OPERATIONS
(SUBJECT TO VARIATION IF FOUND ADVISABLE).

August 27th - Tuesday.
Setting out line for channel and lengths of blasts and fixing positions of dumps for explosives, etc.

August 28th - Wednesday.
Transporting plant and material up to the shore to a base convenient for boats to convey same across the Alt.

August 29th - Thursday.
About 8.0 a.m. start sinking charges of explosives.
About 9.30 a.m. 1st blast about 50 yards long with charges of 22lbs., at suitable distances apart on West Bank of Alt.
Further similar blasts in continuation of first blast at intervals of about 1½ hours up to (say) 4.0 p.m.

It is hoped to cut a channel 200 yards into the sandbank before the flood tide stops the work for the day.

August 30th - Friday.
Further extension of channel by blasting as before; 1st blast (say) about 10.0 a.m. with further blasts at intervals of about 1½ hours up to about 5.0 p.m. It is then expected that the last of the flood tide will flow up the new channel, and the first of the ebb-tide will flow out through it.

August 31st - Saturday.
Further blasts will be made to extend the new channel, and it is hoped to get the Alt flowing through it. Unless the conditions that ensue are very unfavourable, it is expected that the tidal scour will gradually widen the new channel and assist in keeping it open as a new channel for the Alt.

If this desirable end is achieved, the old channel will gradually fill up, but measures would be advisable to accelerate this.

The explosions and progress of the operations should be visible from the sandhills.

The Police have notice to exclude all unauthorised persons from the sandbank on the West side of the Alt, as a necessary precaution and to facilitate the work.

The scheme has been worked out by Mr. H. Treleaven Reade, Surveyor, of 2 South John Street, Liverpool, who is in charge of the operations. Mr. J.A.Wright, the Surveyor to the Council, and Mr. R. Eaton, the Land Drainage Engineer to the County Council, are associated with Mr. H.T.Reade in carrying out the work.

FRANK D. FOULKES,
Clerk to the Great Crosby U.D.C.

Town Hall, Gt.Crosby.
20th Aug. 1929.

A few years later, with the erosion still getting worse, there was a greater danger of Burbo Bank Road also being eroded so another scheme was proposed for diverting the river. A long revetment wall (situated just south of Crosby Sewer) was constructed of heavy waste material obtained from a Bootle foundry, which diverted the river in a westerly direction and away from the sandhills. This has enabled Crosby Corporation to put in hand various schemes for reclamation of the shore which are in various stages of construction at present.
However, there has been no let up in the sand blowing along the shore from Formby into the river, which results in the river encroaching nearer the sandhills, and the various bends getting more pronounced. The bend adjoining the Blundellsands Sailing Club is much worse than it was a while ago and is getting nearer their Pavilion every day as well moving south along the shore. This is where the danger of inundation from a west or south west gale combined with a 31ft tide is at its worst. At present a breakthrough would flood many acres of low ground on both sides of the railway from Moss Lane to Sniggery and beyond. The Dibb Lane area and almost up to the back gardens of Little Crosby Village would not be immune, nor would the new school in the St. Michael's and Manor Road region which is very much below the high water mark. The areas are entirely dependent on the sandhill barrier adjoining the shore for their safety from flooding. This sandhill barrier from Hall Road to Hightown is gradually disappearing and due partially to tide erosion, but mostly through wind erosion which is aggravated very much by the day trippers. Their activities, and in particular the jumping and climbing on the hilltops by the younger trippers, destroy the vegetation, thus allowing the strong winds to erode the loose sand and I am afraid that very soon there will be no sandhill barrier left. The whole coastal area between Hall Road and Hightown will be left without any protection whatsoever from the elements.

It has to remembered that this area of South West Lancashire is wide open to the ravages of the Irish Sea, reinforced (as needs be) by the full force of the North Atlantic and beyond, and no risk should be taken in recognising this fact. With no sandhill barrier left and coastal protection works uncompleted I am of the opinion that to contemplate any development such as a housing estate would be almost criminal and the best thing is to transfer it all back to the green belt from which I am certain it should never have been taken. There is also ample scope for a Nature Reserve to be encouraged in the Fort Crosby area with most of the essentials already on site. I would hazard a guess that this contemplated development scheme was either proposed by some authority who had no idea of coastal difficulties and local history or, alternatively, did not care as long as their development got approval.

In closing, I must mention that in our coastal area some hundreds of years ago the villages of Argarmeols and Ravenmeols, and on our own doorstep the village of Altmouth, were wiped out by an invasion of the sea and who is to say we could not have a repetition. We have no guarantee that a similar catastrophe could not happen again and this leads me to the conviction that the coastal sandhill barrier should be preserved at all costs and even added to in depth. It should never be allowed (as at present) to be slowly demolished by the tidal and wind erosion, the latter of which is so much aggravated by the trippers in the area.

CHAPTER ELEVEN

The Railway

When I first travelled on the railway in about 1897 the trains were, of course, steam trains on the Lancashire and Yorkshire Railway, and we came from Bank Hall to Hightown to stay with relatives who lived in the School Cottages in School Road. The return fare for an adult was ten-pence in real money, and the journey took about 25 minutes. There were the same number of stations as at present, (the only addition between Liverpool and Southport being Hillside in about the 1920s).

The carriages on the trains were lower than at present. Evidence of this can be seen at the Southport end of Hightown Station where the present platform slopes down to a lower level which was the height of the old carriages. The lighting of both the trains and the stations was very poor, being for the most part oil lamps. About 1905 a big alteration work took place and the whole system was electrified, the third rail supplying the current was one of the first of its type to be used.

29. Hightown Railway Station

The station opened on 21st July 1848, and is still in use. Originally there were ladies' and gentlemens' toilets on both sides of the station as well as ladies' and general waiting rooms. There was also a station at Altcar Rifle Range, (called Hightown Rifle Station until July 1886) which opened in 1862, temporarily closed in 1893, re-opened the following year, and finally closed on 3rd October 1921

The change was dramatic and by now I was using trains more often. The twenty minutes service between Liverpool and Southport was maintained from 5.00 a.m. until midnight and catered for the big increase in suburban development along the line. It was a fine service, run for the benefit of the travellers. The buildings and platforms were clean and well lighted. Fires were lit in the waiting rooms during cold weather and the staff planted flowers on the platforms. Waterloo Station was particularly fine with the name of the station planted out with lobelia and alyssum on the embankments either side of the platforms.

30. Bridge construction works, 1967

CHAPTER TWELVE

The Estate

I think it would be some time in 1909, or thereabouts, that the old Squire, William Joseph Blundell, who lived in the Hall at Little Crosby, died and was succeed by Francis Nicholas Blundell.

This brought about many changes and the mortgage solicitors, Guscote, Wadham, Bradbury and Tickle, together with Mr Wright, their Surveyor (who at that time lived in "Glen Allen", Alt Road, Hightown) terminated their interest in the Estate. Mr William Reade, whose father T. Mellard Reade, had formerly administered the Estate, now took over as Surveyor and Messrs Weld and Weld, Solicitors, of Castle Street, Liverpool took over the legal side.

As far as Hightown was concerned, this was a great improvement, for both Mr Reade and Mr Francis Weld had a great local interest in the district.

At this time my father had negotiated with the mortgage solicitors a scheme for the development of School Road and part of Lower Alt Road consisting of six terraced houses, a shop, and a further terrace of nine houses which finished opposite the Bank in Lower Alt Road. He was about half way through completing the first six houses in this scheme when the change-over occurred.

Mr Reade's first job was to produce a plan for developing the area of Lower Alt Road and Thornbeck Avenue and clearing the sand dunes but never lower than 26ft O.D. - this being the level of the kerb in Lower Alt Road. The bench mark cut into the kerb still remains on the south side of the road opposite "Kirk Bank". Mr Reade was emphatic that this level was just 9'6" above a 31ft tide and for safety was a minimum that could be allowed, provided the range of high sandhills along the tide line was preserved until a more permanent protection was built at Blundellsands.

This new plan of Mr Reade meant some alteration to my father's scheme, the outcome of which was that the house where I now live was built by my father for himself, instead of a shop as originally planned. Then two pairs of semi-detached houses took the place of the nine terraced houses. The second pair of semis were ground floor high when a tenant of Little Crosby Village, Mr Charles Russell, persuaded Mr F. N. Blundell to convert them into shops which he then bought. They are now the present Post Office.

At this time I was only 19 years old and trying to make myself useful on the building site. So when Mr Reade asked my father for the use of my services to help him with his surveying, by holding his tape and staff, I was only too willing to help. He had me fix second-hand railway sleepers on end in the hollows of the sandhills and cut off at 26ft O.D. as a guide for levelling and clearing sand for when development started.

31. "The Luff", School Road
This was Joe Bulman's residence until his death in 1981. Joe's father built it shortly before the 1st World War

Roughly speaking, his proposed lay-out of the Thornbeck area consisted of Thornbeck Avenue running parallel to the shore nearly to Fort Crosby. Then it went in a south-easterly direction, crossing the railway near to Sniggery, then across the field skirting that part of the West Lancs. Golf Club which was then on the east side of the railway, and carried on to join Little Crosby Road, in the vicinity of Boundary Cottage. This was to be the main road into Hightown with dual-carriageways and central grassed area, as can be seen in the first 100 yards or so of Thornbeck Avenue.

Mr Reade was convinced there would be no large scale development of the east side of this railway at Hightown due to sewer and drainage problems. He maintained that Moss Lane and Alt Road would adequately cope with the traffic for this part of Hightown. He was satisfied that the new development could begin at Sniggery on both sides of Thornbeck Avenue, without bringing all the site traffic into Hightown Village - as the new developers have done - and there would be no necessity for the Kerslake Way shambles on the ramp bridge at the Station, which is such a nuisance to all Hightown, in particular the elderly and mothers with prams and young children.

Clearance of the area was very slow until the late 1930s when the West Lancs. Brick Co. Ltd., whose factory was sited where Hester Close now is, had cleared the sand to the north of their factory, being roughly the Mark Road area. These levels of 26ft O.D. were strictly observed under the direction of Mr Reade, and it was ready for the development which has now taken place on this site. A start was made on the Thornbeck Avenue area, but shortly afterwards, the outbreak of the Second World War saw the closure of the brickworks, and consequently the clearing of the sand ended. Then unfortunately Mr Reade died in 1940 and nobody was left to supervise. The bombing of the towns and cities started about now and the call came for sand to fill sandbags to protect public buildings. All observance of Mr Reade's levels was ignored and sand was taken indiscriminately from wherever it was most convenient. There was no supervision as it was a state of emergency. In my opinion, the entire site was left in 1945 not much higher than the highest tide and without much protection and not fit for development.

Considering this lay-out was surveyed about 1908-10 and the internal combustion engine had not yet inflicted the devastation it has done since, and the motor car has caused such congestion, this was a very far-seeing development and has a lot of advantages over the present one.

32. Lower Alt Road
The shops were (left to right) Mr Corn the Cobbler, Mrs Edwards' furnishing shop, David Edwards' shop and Rawsthorne's (furniture, carpets, soft furnishings). Rawsthorne's also had a shop on College Road, Great Crosby. The car in the photo is an Austin A40, Mk 1, introduced in September 1958.

CHAPTER THIRTEEN

Footpath to Formby

From my earliest memories of Hightown, one of the most enjoyable was walking across the Rifle Range to Cabin Hill to bathe.

We kids used a footpath that went along the River Alt bank from the bottom of Lower Alt Road, up to the brick flood-gates bridge across the river. It then followed the cinder paths in the Camp and out to Cabin Hill, and if no firing, to a short cut across the ranges, through the old Battery and on to the shore.

The sand and sea were clean, and of course, we had the shore to ourselves. About 1910-12 a gamekeeper named Peter Cullen, employed by the Earl of Sefton, came to live in Grange Cottages. He was responsible for the Earl of Sefton erecting a wire netting fence along what was then the boundary between Blundell of Crosby Estate and the Earl of Sefton Estate. Part of this boundary is now the fence between Numbers 15 and 17 Mark Road. Later there was an exchange of land, the Earl of Sefton taking the part of the Blundell of Crosby land south of his boundary but west of the River Alt. In exchange the Blundell of Crosby Estate took the land north of this boundary up to the fence that marks the south of the Rifle Range, just beyond the Mark Road bungalows.

33. Hightown Cross
An evocative image, sketched in the first half of the 19th century. (Reproduced courtesy of Manchester Public Libraries).

Peter Cullen was ably assisted by John Munro, then Range Manager, and we were convinced that the sole purpose of this fence was to provide a private rabbit shooting course, for they could often be seen out with their guns and dogs.

An uneasy peace existed for a number of years. Occasionally an employee of the Rifle Range would try to be a little awkward, but by and large we continued to walk across the Range to Cabin Hill, or to Andrew's Lane, Formby. My father warned the gamekeeper that any attempt to close the right of way, by locking the gate in the fence, would be challenged by the Footpaths and Commons Association.

Then in 1933/4 the West Lancs. Territorial Association closed the gate in the fence and stopped the footpath. This brought immediate action from some of the Hightown residents backed by the Hightown Ratepayers' Association, residents from Formby, Altcar and the Ramblers' Association. I helped, with other locals, in much research into the rights of way through Hightown and statements were taken from several old residents. There is no doubt that a right of way existed and was used many, many years ago by fishermen who carried their catches to Liverpool. Research proved that the old footpath from Liverpool to Formby, long before the railway, was along the Leeds and Liverpool Canal tow-path to Derwent Road, Endbutt Lane, Liverpool Road, Cooks Road, Manor Road, Hall Road East, across three fields to Sniggery, Gorsey Lane, Dobb Lane, Sandy Lane, and from somewhere about the site of the cross at "Cross House", diagonally through the sandhills to the flood-gates bridge crossing the Alt, through to Cabin Hill and Formby Point. The other path finished along the Alt Kop to Andrew's Lane.

The bridge at the flood-gates was repaired and restored in 1896 by my father. The original brick bridge was thought to be at least 100 years old then, for the English oak gates had worn out and that would take some time to happen. It was thought to be part of the scheme to prevent tidal flooding higher up the River Alt. I have in my possession a photograph taken in 1896 of this restoration work in progress.

I just remember, when very young, the 'ride over'. This was the day when all the landowners with property depending on the Alt for drainage - the Earl of Sefton, Lord Derby, Squire of Ince Blundell, Squire Blundell of Little Crosby, and perhaps others attended by their agents - rode on horse-back along the banks of the Alt from Knowsley up to the floodgates. Here they turned east to cross the railway through a wicket gate close to Altcar Rifle Range Station, and then on to what was Barnes' Pub (now The Pheasant) for lunch. From here, they carried on home by road.

APPENDIX 1

Footpaths Dispute

In 1937 a dispute arose regarding the West Lancashire Territorial Army Association's closure of two footpaths which led from Hightown to Formby across land occupied by the Altcar Rifle Range. One of these footpaths was said to be the old fishermen's bridle path from the Formby shore to Liverpool. These paths had been illegally closed in March 1933 and on Good Friday 1934 respectively. In 1937 the Hightown Ratepayers' Association, enforced by a petition signed by 60 residents of Hightown, took up the matter with the Ramblers' Association (Liverpool & District Federation Footpaths Committee) who sent the petition to the County Council. The text of the petition was as follows:

Path "A"

From Alt Cottage, North-End Lane to Grange Farm.

This path was illegally closed in March 1933.

A brick cottage was built on the Alt side of the LMS railway line to house a gate-keeper in the employ of the West Lancashire Territorial Army Association, who had written instructions from Major H.R. Parkes to turn back all pedestrians except those carrying a permit from him or having business on the Altcar Rifle Range.

The closure of this path was brought to our notice several times during the summer of 1933 by members of our Association who were prevented by the gate-keeper from continuing along this public path to Formby.

We wrote to Major Parkes, and he replied that it was "a private way belonging to the Croxteth Estates". We thereupon wrote to the Croxteth Estates Office, and were informed by Mr T.W. Haward that this was a "private, gated accommodation road to Grange Farm" and that it was "specifically referred to as a private road in the conveyance (dated July 30 1912) of the Rifle Range, by Lord Sefton to the Territorial Association".

We maintain that although this is a private road for vehicles, there is also a public right of way for pedestrians over it.

We have interviewed many of the oldest inhabitants of Hightown and district, and they assert that they have always had free and uninterrupted use of this public path until March 1933.

The only restriction of any sort on this path was a charge of 1/- levied by Mr Ruston (tenant of Grange Farm) on all vehicles using the road from Cleaver Cottages across the LMS railway, through Grange Farm yard, and over the iron bridge by the old lighthouse on to the Rifle Range. This was the charge for keeping the road and bridge in order and repair, and was collected for him by Mr Seddon who lived in an old cottage in North End Lane which was demolished for the erection of Cleaver Cottages. Several sons have signed the attached petition, and in their young days they collected the tolls for their mother and are willing to be interviewed on the subject. They will confirm that at no time was any obstruction or restriction or charge placed on pedestrians, in fact a wicket gate was installed at the main road entrance for their greater convenience, together with two other wicket gates, one at each side of the railway crossing. These wicket gates were never fitted with locks.

As Mr Ruston's tenancy of the farm terminated about 1904, continual use of this public footpath for the last fifty years is shown in the above evidence.

After closing Path "A" in 1933, the West Lancashire Territorial Association turned their attention to the second path "B" in 1934.

PATH "B"

This runs on the east bank of the River Alt from Lower Alt Road, Hightown, and passes through a gate in the Rifle Range boundary fence.

This gate was fitted with a lock by the West Lancashire Territorial Association, and so closed for the first time in history on Good Friday, 1934.

The inhabitants of the neighbourhood were indignant at this unprecedented action, and brought the matter to the attention of the West Lancashire Rural District Council.

This Council then passed a resolution on 9th April 1935, denying that this path was a public right of way. When this became known, local residents placed certain evidence before the Council for their meeting on 18th July 1935, with a request that they should rescind their resolution of 9th April. The Council subsequently appointed a sub-committee to consider the matter, and we understand this committee did meet some officials of the WLTAA but did not rescind their resolution.

During 1936 the Ramblers' Federation (Liverpool & District Branch) in collaboration with local residents, have collected further evidence from old users of these paths.

We possess testimony from 60 people who have used the path for periods ranging from 20 to 65 years and whose fathers used it before them, always without let or hindrance.

We attach a copy of this evidence to our letter.

In addition we would draw attention to the following points:-

> *This path is a very ancient public right of way. History has it that in the old days when cockle fishing thrived at Formby, this path was the fishermen's bridle path to Liverpool, and was in existence long before the present main road at North End, and even before Hightown existed.*
>
> *In the days when this land was let to farmers, their gamekeepers were unable to stop the local people carrying guns over the land on this path, because it was a public right of way.*
>
> *The canteen on the Rifle Range always had a full 12 months' licence. It would seem to be very remarkable that a public house with a 12 months' licence should be situated in the centre of what the WLTAA claim to be private ground. After the camping season was over, i.e. between October and Easter, there would be no trade whatsoever for this licence if the civilian customers had no right of way by which to reach the fully licenced premises. The postal delivery to Cabin Hill Farm, situated outside the Rifle Range land on the northern boundary, is from Hightown Post Office, and the postman uses this public right of way across the Rifle Range.*
>
> *The two gates at the northern ends of this path have not been locked by the WLTAA. They are open at all times now, as indeed they have always been; but at weekends only, and in the summer only, the WLTAA station an employee at each gate to prevent the public entering these paths from the Formby end. This seems like a queer sort of business if there is no right of way through them. All traffic for the Rifle Range is either via Grange Farm for road users, or via the LMS footpath from Hightown to Altcar Rifle Range Station.*
>
> *This path is the only way from Hightown to Formby, except the main road, which is at present a death trap for pedestrians, the footwalks being narrow and hardly usable, and the road being narrow and winding and crowded with traffic from Liverpool, Bootle and Crosby to Formby, Freshfield, Ainsdale and Southport. Moreover, this poor, alternative, main road route adds two miles to the journey from Hightown to Formby and vice versa.*

In these circumstances, therefore, we submit copies of our evidence to the County Council as the Highways Authority.

We feel confident that after examining the case we now put forward, the County Council will use its influence to bring about a reconsideration of the matter and so restore to the inhabitants of Hightown and Formby, and to the public generally, their ancient rights of way.

The ensuing public enquiry, instituted by the County Council, was held at the Hightown Hotel on 6th April 1937.

Mr A.D. Dean, representing the petitioners (the Ramblers' Association, the Hightown Ratepayers' Association, and a number of local residents) said there was "an extraordinary volume of evidence" that an unrestricted right of way had existed over the footpaths for many years. They had been illegally closed in recent years (i.e. since 1933) by the West Lancashire Territorial Army Association (WLTAA) but the provisions of the Military Act 1892 and the Highways and Town Planning Acts had not been followed. Mr Dean then called numerous witnesses who gave evidence to the effect that for many years (some witnesses going back to 1875) these paths had been recognised as public rights of way.

The Alt Catchment Board's representative was concerned with the right of way over the sluice and floodgates which linked the footpaths on each side of the river. When the Range was conveyed to the WLTAA in 1912, a clause in the conveyance stated that there was no right of way over the bridge. In 1913 an agreement was entered into with the Commissioners of the River Alt and the WLTAA giving the Territorials a right of way over the bridge as owners of the land. In effect, the position was that the bridge could be closed by the Commissioners without any reason being given.

Mr Selwyn Lloyd on behalf of the WLTAA, related how in 1928 the number of people going on the land was so great that the Association thought action should be taken. At first a wicket gate was closed, but as this proved ineffective other means of closing the land were employed. It was claimed that certain selected individuals, or class of individuals, used to go on the land and these were responsible persons who were known to the owners. The contract between the WLTAA and Lord Sefton drawn up in 1912 did not mention any rights of way across the land and the Territorial Association had no power to create a right of way.

It was pointed out by Mr Dean, at the conclusion of the enquiry, that the petitioners had no objection to the footpaths being fenced and had tried to seek a compromise with the WLTAA but had been blankly refused.

The outcome of the enquiry was that an arrangement was reached whereby the WLTAA would provide a new footpath along the west side of the railway adjoining the Rifle Range in substitution for the foot paths which the Association desired to close to the general public. A fence would be erected alongside the footpath and two small culvert bridges and a bridge across the River Alt would be provided. The County Council made a contribution to the expense of these alterations.

APPENDIX 2
Hightown Miscellany

Hightown Cross

Hightown Cross is thought to be the first of five crosses at approximately one-mile intervals, from the coast to Sefton Church. On this stretch of coast the bodies of shipwrecked sailors would be washed ashore, and there was a mortuary in the sand hills to house them. The funeral cortège would then proceed to the burial ground at Sefton, resting at the crosses, and the mourners would take refreshment at the inn which was usually opposite. There used to be an inn by the cross in Hightown.

The cross is about two feet above the present pavement and set in a sandstone pedestal. It dates from the 19th century, but the pedestal is much older. According to Henry Taylor in 'Ancient Crosses and Holy Wells of Lancashire': "A new cross, with floriated terminations, similar in character to that at Ince Blundell, was placed in the old socket about the year 1880 by the late Colonel Blundell. The old one was destroyed by some drunken men." An unsubstantiated story has it that some men returning from target practice at Altcar rifle Range damaged the cross.

Crosby Lighthouse

The first Crosby Lighthouse was built in 1839, and became operational on 10th October of that year. It was a wooden structure, and exhibited a red fixed light, 96 feet above the half tide level. The light was visible for sixteen miles. The lighthouse was used in conjunction with Formby Lighthouse which was about one-and-a-half miles away.

The first Crosby Lighthouse lasted only until 1847 when a second was built about half a mile away; this commenced operations on 2nd November of that year. The second lighthouse was mostly constructed of bricks and had a square tapering tower. The lighthouse stood approximately 600 yards from the Truant School.

This lighthouse was destroyed by fire in 1898. Approximately ten years before, there had been another fire at the lighthouse which was put out by the keeper and his wife. At that time there had been seven lamps in the lighthouse, but after the fire the number was reduced to five, and more ventilation put in the building.

Railway Bridge

British Rail announced in November 1964 the construction of a passenger and traffic bridge to span the Liverpool-Southport railway line, shortly afterwards, work started. The bridge replaced level crossing gates at Hightown Station: these were closed down in March 1967, and the road bridge was opened shortly afterwards.

34. Hightown War Memorial
The memorial was unveiled on 11th November 1920 by Mr T.H. Russell J.P., chairman of Little Crosby Council

35. Remembrance Day 1968
Dr D.R. Williams lays a wreath at Hightown war memorial, watched by Canon Francis Danher, Parish Priest of Our Lady of Victories RC Church

After the closure of the crossing gates there was a long-running public protest backed by the Crosby Herald and the local MP, Graham Page. The problem was pedestrian access over the railway line; they could either use the existing footbridge which had over fifty steep steps, and was therefore impractical for the elderly and those with young children, or use the new road bridge which was quite a distance away from the station, and busy with traffic. Residents complained about Hightown being split in two, and shops such as Gaffney's found their takings significantly down. Eventually the present footbridge, which includes a gently sloping ramp, was built. This was completed in April 1972 at the cost of £15,000; British Rail made a £500 donation, and Crosby Borough Council paid the rest.

Hightown's War Memorials

The village's principal war memorial was unveiled on 11th November 1920 by Mr T.H. Russell, J.P., chairman of Little Crosby Urban District Council. At the ceremony children placed wreaths on the memorial, and the Last Post was sounded. The memorial is constructed of Bath stone and Dutch bricks.

There was some controversy about the war memorial in the early 1980s, as to who should maintain it. The memorial was showing signs of erosion, but Sefton Council claimed never to have been responsible for it, and the general opinion was that residents of Hightown had paid it for. However Sefton Council does now have responsibility for it and the memorial has been restored to its original splendour.

There is also a war memorial at St. Stephen's Church, unveiled on Sunday 9th September 1923. The tablet is of bronze and was placed in the west wall of the church. Another memorial is at the Hightown Club, unveiled on 30th August 1919 by Captain F.N. Blundell. In his speech, reported by the Crosby Herald, Captain Blundell said: "...the 'Boys' had played cricket to the last, and no honour, however great, could adequately repay them for the great sacrifice they had rendered for the protection of our homes and country."

St. Stephen's Church

Plans for Hightown Mission Church were drawn up at the beginning of the 20th century by Shepheard & Bower, Architects, of Liverpool. The church, named St. Stephen's, came into being in 1914, the foundation stone being laid by Mrs R. Rainshaw Rothwell, wife of the patron of the living of Sefton, on 17th July. At the beginning of 1971 St. Stephen's became a parish church in its own right, reflecting the increase in its congregation; prior to that it had been part of the parish of St. Nicholas', Blundellsands.

Our Lady of Victories Church

The church was completed in 1916 and opened on May 7th of that year. Prior to the church's creation, services were held in a building belonging to Mr Gregg (builder) on St. Georges Road, the hut being cleared at weekends for services. Originally Roman Catholics in Hightown had to travel to St. Mary's Church in Little Crosby. Our Lady of Victories remained part of that parish until 1924, when it was separated off.

The porch and vestry were added after the 2nd World War. The church did not get a parish hall until July 1977; prior to that, social events were held in the hall of St. Stephen's Church. The main problem with building the hall was the lack of space available, as there was only a small triangular piece of land alongside the church. Mike Williams the architect, a parishioner at the church, overcame this problem by incorporating the triangle-shape as a feature of the design. The new hall cost £18,000.

Alt Grange

Altcar Grange was built in the 13th century by monks from Stanlaw Abbey, on land given to them by William Blundell of Ince Blundell. The monks left during the Reformation. In 1543 the Grange was sold to Richard Molyneux of West Derby and for two hundred years it was a gentleman's residence. Molyneux was a Roman Catholic, and the Grange had at least one priest's hiding hole. The family appear to have died off by 1734. The novel 'A Jacobite Conspiracy' by 19th century writer Mrs G Norway describes the Grange at this time, with particular reference to smuggling.

Until 1859 the Grange was owned by the Earl of Sefton and occupied by tenant farmers. Then the West Lancashire Territorial Army ran the land as a rifle range for local volunteers. In 1908 the lease was £1,744 p.a.(in 1859 it had been £170). Therefore in 1913, the Territorial Army decided to buy the Grange and 1,200 acres from Lord Sefton for £92,000

J.H. Williams, artist

John Henry Williams (sometimes known as Harry Williams) was active 1845-77. He was a landscape painter and, according to the Walker Art Gallery catalogue, "said to be the son of a Liverpool tradesman".

He was born in Liverpool, and lived there until about 1856. He resided at various addresses in the city including Simcock Street which was in the Toxteth Park area, Williamson Square, Bedford Street North and Brownlow Street. He married the daughter of a Liverpool publican, and they had a son, also called Harry. Williams moved to London in 1856, and then about 1873, to Penzance in Cornwall. He ended his life back in London where he died in poverty.

John Henry Williams exhibited at the Liverpool Academy 1845-58, Royal Academy 1856, Society of British Artists 1854-77 and the Liverpool Autumn Exhibition 1874-76. "Near Altcar" was purchased for the Walker from Alfred Kind in 1906.

His early paintings were mostly landscapes of Merseyside, Cheshire and Wales. Later on in his career he roved further afield and his landscapes included subjects in Sussex, Northumbria, Norfolk and Ireland. John Henry Williams was never a well-known painter and information on him is scarce. A further complication is that some works attributed to him may have been by his son Harry, who was also an artist.

APPENDIX 3

The Hightown War Memorial

by Hal Giblin

The Hightown War Memorial was designed - and its erection supervised and overseen - by Architect, Trenwith Lovering Wills, whose younger brother,Second Lieutenant John Godfrey Wills, Royal Field Artillery, had been killed in France on 27 September 1918. The boys' father, John Trenwith Wills, who managed the Press Association office in Liverpool had brought his wife and sons to live in Hightown from their former home in Tranmere several years before the start of the Great War. The Wills family lived in one of the comparatively few houses built entirely of the distinctively beige-coloured 'Hightown' brick. The house name in those days was obviously chosen to reflect its appearance: *'Buff House'*! (now 'Westmount', 1 Blundell Road).

The younger son, John, a member of the Hightown Club and a cricketer of some ability, worked in the offices of Blessig, Braun and Company, Commission Merchants in Rumford Place, Liverpool. He was amongst the very first to enlist when war came and, on 8 August 1914 - only four days after the official declaration - was accepted as a Driver into 4th West Lancashire, Royal Field Artillery. John first went to France in August 1915, and soon distinguished himself. In November 1916, he was sent home to attend an Officers course at the Royal Artillery Cadet School at St. Johns Wood. John was commissioned 24 April 1917 and posted to Woolwich. He was again sent to the front in August 1918, where he was attached to 'A' Battery, 93rd Brigade, Royal Field Artillery. On the last day of his young life, less than six weeks before the war's end, John was acting as Forward Observation Officer for his Brigade during the attack on the Canal du Nord, near Moeuvres - a hazardous appointment indeed. In a letter to his grief stricken mother, his Commanding Officer, Lieutenant Colonel Charles Gower wrote, '*....they were close behind the infantry and had gained the opposite bank of the canal, when a machine-gun turned upon them, killing your poor son. Had he survived I would have had the pleasure of recommending him for the Military Cross*'.

The older brother, Trenwith, then working in London as an Architect, enlisted as a Trooper in the 1st County of London Yeomanry on 12 September 1914. He served with his regiment in Gallipoli for two months between August and October 1915, before being struck down with enteric fever and evacuated from that terrible Peninsular. After recovering his health, he was commissioned Second Lieutenant in the Essex Yeomanry on 18 January 1916. His training as an Architect proved valuable to the army and he was transferred from the Yeomanry to the Royal Artillery in March 1918. His technical abilities probably saved his life for he was never asked to go overseas again. In later life, Trenwith Wills would practise as an Architect in partnership with a member of that most distinguished of British military families, a Wellesley.

Who better to design and oversee the building of the Memorial which would serve to commemorate not only his own dear brother, but all the Hightown men who made the supreme sacrifice in the Great War and in wars still then to come?

One of John Will's fellow officers who was also a personal friend, wrote to Mrs Wills after her son's death in action: ***'One more life nobly sacrificed for the cause of liberty and right is one more name on that wonderful scroll, which future generations will uphold forever'***.

I, for one, trust that he will prove correct in that prediction....

HIGHTOWN WAR MEMORIAL
The Great War

George **Bradshaw,** Private (Number 36709) 10th Battalion, Royal North Lancashire Regiment, killed in action during the Third Battle of Ypres on 7 October 1917. No known grave, commemorated on the Tyn Cot Memorial, Passchendaele, Belgium. Aged 20. The son of Mrs Jane Bradshaw of 1 Cleaver Cottages, Hightown. *(Also (George HENRY Bradshaw) on Formby Memorial and 'Our Lady of Compassion' Memorial, Formby).*

John **Bullen**, Private (Number 42864) 6th Battalion, Leicestershire Regiment, killed in action in the final advance on 18 September 1918. Buried in Villers Hill British Cemetery, France. Aged 18. Son of Mr and Mrs David Bullen of Haycut Cottages, St. George's Road, Hightown. *(Also on Ince Blundell Memorial).*

Harold **Crompton,** Pioneer (Number 49916) 154th Field Company, Royal Engineers, killed in action on the first day of the Battle of the Somme, 1 July 1916. Buried in Bienvillers Military Cemetery, France. Aged 21. Son of Joseph and Barbara Crompton of 5, Bungalow, Hightown. (Native of Bolton). *(Residence was one of a group of wooden bungalows on the sandhills on the left of Lower Alt Road - demolished prior to the development of 'Riverside'.*

James **Hampson,** Private (Number 276861) 17th Manchester Regiment. Killed in action 29 March 1918. No known grave and therefore commemorated on the Arras Memorial, France. Born, lived and enlisted in Liverpool. Formerly No. 35464 Liverpool Regiment.

Percy **Lancaster**, Second Lieutenant, 17th (Pals) Battalion, King's Liverpool Regiment and 122nd Battalion, Machine Gun Corps (Infantry) killed in action in the Battle of Flers-Courcelette on the Somme, 15 September 1916. No known grave, commemorated on the Thiepval Memorial, France. Lived at Beach Cottage, Hightown. *(Also on the bronze plaque Memorial in the body of St. Stephen's Church).*

James Lawrence **Kenny**, Master Mariner, SS *Asturias*, Mercantile Marine, died 21st August 1918 at Murmansk, Russia and is buried in Murmansk New British Cemetery, Russian Federation. Husband of Sarah Josephine Kenny of 'The Homestead', Hightown. *(The Asturias (Royal Mail Steam Packet Co.) - 12,002 tons - was taken over by the Admiralty for service as a hospital ship. On 20 March 1917, after safely landing wounded soldiers from the Salonika front at Avonmouth, the Asturias was steaming up the Channel with all lights burning and the Red Cross on her side clearly visible, when she was torpedoed by a German submarine 6 miles off Start Point. The explosion killed several men outright and the total deaths amounted to 45, including doctors and nurses. The Asturias was run ashore at Bolt Head, eventually refloated and brought back into service. It is not known whether Kenny was Master of the Asturias at the time of this incident). Also commemorated on the Crosby Memorial and the St. Peter and Paul Memorial, Crosby (formerly lived at 8 Kimberley Drive, Great Crosby).*

Percival Frederick **Owen**, Gunner (Number 681463) "D" Battery, 160th Brigade, Royal Field Artillery, killed in action in the battle of Lys, on 19 April 1918. Buried in Veille-Chapelle New Military Cemetery, Lacouture, France. Aged 24. Son of William and Mary Elizabeth Owen of "Lynton", School Road, Hightown. *(Also on the bronze plaque Memorial in the body of St. Stephen's Church).*

Joseph **Rainford**, Private (Number 54265) 2/5th Battalion, Lancashire Fusiliers, killed in action during a German counter attack on a position at Ere, near Tournai, Belgium on 25 October 1918. Buried in Tournai Communal Cemetery, Allied Extension, Belgium. Aged 21. Son of John and Jane Rainford of Wood Farm, Hightown. *(Also commemorated on the St. Mary's Memorial, Little Crosby).*

James Stanley **Riding**, Private (Number 15470) 17th (Pals) Battalion, The King's Liverpool Regiment, died of wounds received at Maricourt during the first day of the Battle of the Somme. 1 July 1916. Buried in La Neuville Communal Cemetery (Corbie), France. Aged 20. Son of James and Grace Riding of "Innisfallen", School Road, Hightown. *(Commemorated on the bronze plaque Memorial in the body of St. Stephen's Church). N.B. James Riding Senior was also the grandfather of Ronald Joseph Baybut - killed in the Second World War (see below)). (Several family members still living in Hightown).*

Arthur John **Scott**, Private (Number 2577) "A" Company, 10th (Scottish) Battalion, The King's Liverpool Regiment - "The Liverpool Scottish" - killed in action in the area of Hill 60 on the Ypres Salient, Belgium, on 17 March 1915. Buried in Perth Cemetery (China Wall), Belgium. Aged 21. The son of William Robert and Ada Maud Scott of School Road, Hightown. *(Commemorated on the bronze plaque Memorial in the body of St. Stephen's Church AND on St Stephen's brass Altar Cross which has the following inscription:* ***"To the Glory of God and in Loving Memory of Arthur John Scott 10th (Scottish) Battn. K.L.R. who was killed in action near Ypres 17th March 1915. Greater Love Hath No Man Than This"****). (Arthur's sisters, Ivy and Christabel (Chrissie), subsequently moved from School Road to Rathbone Road).*

John Godfrey **Wills**, Second Lieutenant, "A" Battery, 93rd Brigade, Royal Field Artillery, killed in action on the first day of the attack on the Canal du Nord on 27 September 1918. Buried in Louverval Military Cemetery, Doignies, France. Aged 25. The son of John Trenwith Wills and Florence Wills of 1, Blundell Road, Hightown. *(Commemorated on the bronze plaque Memorial in the body of St. Stephen's Church and on the Hightown Club Memorial). (John's brother, Trenwith Wills, was the architect of the Hightown War Memorial).*

Also - NOT commemorated on the Hightown Memorial:-

John McCurdy **Gregg**, Private (Number 357124) 1/10th (Scottish) Battalion, The King's Liverpool Regiment - "The Liverpool Scottish" - died in a Military Hospital on 11 May 1918, of wounds received earlier in the trenches near Givenchy, France. Buried in Etaples Military Cemetery, France. Aged 39. Son of Samuel J. and Mrs Gregg of Hightown; husband of Agnes M. Gregg of Gable House, Formby. (Native of Co. Down, Ireland). Formby Times, 18 May 1918: *'The Officer Commanding St. John's Hospital, Etaples, France, advises that John McCurdy Gregg of the Liverpool Regiment, eldest son of Mr & Mrs Gregg of Hightown, died on Sunday 11th inst. of wounds received on 27 April. He was educated at the Liverpool Northern Institute and Formby College. He joined up in 1915 and in the first attack on Guillemont was one of the few who came back'. Also commemorated on the Formby Memorial and the Holy Trinity Memorial, Formby.*

The Second World War

Ronald Joseph **Baybut**, Private (Number 2929880) 7/10th Battalion, Argyll and Sutherland Highlanders, killed in action in the North African Campaign on 6 March 1943. Had served originally with the Gordon Highlanders (1939). Buried in the Enfidaville War Cemetery, Tunisia. Aged 22. Son of Joseph and Grace Ann Baybut of Hightown. *(Commemorated on the Roll of Honour in the porch of St. Stephen's). (N.B. Ronald was the grandson of James Riding Senior, the father of J.S. Riding who was killed in the Great War (see above)). (Several family members still living in Hightown).*

Terence King **Boardman**, Sergeant (Number 565854) 44 Squadron, Royal Air Force, died on active service, 19 June 1941. Buried in Lincoln (Newport) Cemetery, England. Aged 25. Son of Frederic Charles and Maud Mary Boardman of "Holmefield", 14 Blundell Road, Hightown. *(commemorated on the Roll of Honour in the porch of St. Stephen's). (Mr Boardman Senior was the Station Master of Hall Road Station).*

Neil **Buchanan**, Sub-Lieutenant, Royal Naval Volunteer Reserve, killed in action on board the destroyer, H.M.S. *Janus*, on 23 January 1944. H.M.S. *Janus* (Lt. Cdr W B R Morrison) had taken part in the British/American landings at Anzio on 22 January 1944. On the following day, when off Nettuno, she was hit by a torpedo from a German dive bomber and foundered in twenty five minutes, taking with her, her 7 officers (including Neil Buchanan) and 155 ratings. Commemorated on the Portsmouth Naval Memorial, Panel 88, Column 1. Neil was the third son of Ernest and Linda Buchanan of "Ballure", Blundell Road, Hightown. *(Commemorated on the Roll of Honour in the porch of St. Stephen's and on the Waterloo RUFC Memorial and in the United Reformed Church, Warren Road, Blundellsands). (Brother, Colonel Buchanan, lives in Formby).*

James Lowden **Connell**, Acting Sub/Lieutenant (Engineering), Royal Naval Volunteer Reserve. Killed in action aboard H.M.S. *Avenger* on 15 November 1942. H.M.S. *Avenger* (Commander A.P Colthurst), an escort aircraft carrier, was taking part in the North African landings when West of the Straits of Gibralter, she was torpedoed and sunk by a submarine. Sixty-seven officers (including Jimmy Connell) and 438 ratings were killed. This was the heaviest British naval loss connected with the North African landings. Aged 30, the son of Alf Connell and Mrs Connell of "Ennerdale", St. George's Road, Hightown. Commemorated on the Liverpool Naval Memorial Panel 4, Column 1. *(Also commemorated on the Roll of Honour in the porch of St. Stephen's). (His father later took up permanent residence in the Hightown Hotel - he acted as scorer for Hightown Cricket Team and was President of Hightown Club at one time). (Jimmy Connell was the nephew of Sir James Connell, a shipping man and one time Liberal M.P.) (Mrs Connell lived in an open air chalet in the garden - thought to be beneficial for her health - unfortunately, however, she died young) (James's sister, Mary, married a Mr Duxfield and moved to Lathom, near Ormskirk).*

John Reginald **Green**, Gunner (Number 929330). 75th (The Shropshire Yeomanry) Field Regiment, Royal Artillery. Died at Bodesworth Castle, Tattenhall on 20 December 1940. Buried in Sefton Churchyard (grave 14/8). The son of Mr and Mrs J E Green of "Danefield", Alt Road, Hightown.

Michael Cyril **Hebbert**, Lieutenant, 9th Battalion, Durham Light Infantry. Killed in action in northern Holland during the night of 9/10th November 1944. Buried in the British Military Cemetery, Jonkerbos, near Nijmegan, Holland. Aged 23. The youngest of the three sons of Sidney and Alice Hebbert of "Glenalt", Blundell Road, Hightown. B.A. Cantab. (First Class Honours - English Literature Tripos). Said to be the first St. Mary's College Old Boy to go to Cambridge. *(Commemorated on the Roll of Honour in the porch of St. Stephen's and on the St. Aloysius School Memorial, Glasgow and on the St. Mary's College Memorial, Crosby) (N.B. Brother, Tony, lives in Blundellsands. Mother lived to the age of 105!)*

Ronald **Jones**, Pilot Officer (Number 67616) 228 Squadron, Royal Air Force Volunteer Reserve, died on active service on 4 May 1942. Buried in Sefton (St.Helen) Churchyard, England. Aged 28. Son of Samuel and Isabella Jones of Liverpool and husband of Maud Ophelia Jones of Hightown. *(Commemorated on the Roll of Honour in the porch of St. Stephen's).*

Daly Charles **Garton-Stone,** Lieutenant (Air) Royal Navy, killed in action flying off the aircraft carrier, H.M.S. *Illustrious,* on 21 December 1940. H.M.S. *Illustrious* was off the eastern Tunisian coast on 21 December 1940. Two of her Swordfish sank cargo vessels near to Safx, however, one of the planes, piloted by Lieutenant Daly C Garton-Stone, failed to return. Daly was the son of Mr and Mrs Stone of "Sunwards", Thirlmere Road, Hightown. Commemorated on the Fleet Air Arm Memorial, Lee-on-Solent, Hampshire, Bay 1, Panel 2. *(Commemorated on the Roll of Honour in the porch of St.Stephen's and on the Waterloo RUFC Memorial). (Youngest of three children - one brother, Gaton Garton-Stone and a sister, Cherry) (Brother Gaton later lived at "Glenallen", Alt Road, Hightown).*

William **Wilson.** Untraced, however during 1939/1945 a Wilson family lived at "Cintra", Blundell Road, Hightown (William Robert Wilson Snr; William Robert Wilson Jnr; Dorothy Gwendoline Louise Wilson; Elizabeth Jane Wilson - by 1945 BOTH men were no longer listed in the Voters' Register).

James **Wylie.** Captain, Royal Army Chaplains Department. Lived in St.Stephen's Lodge, Lower Alt Road. *(Commemorated on the Roll of Honour in the porch of St.Stephen's). (Graduated from Clifton Theological College in 1932. Dean in 1934. Priest in 1935. Curate of Whitford Mere 1936. Curate at St. Nicholas, Blundellsands, 1936-1939. T.A. Reserve of Chaplains. Appointed Chaplain to the Forces, 29 August 1939 (4th Class, ranking as Captain). Crockford (1941) shows him as being in the Derby Diocese in 1939 and 1940 - does not again appear - therefore died between 1940 and 1947).*

The following MAY be omissions and do not appear on the Hightown Memorial:

(?) **Hall**, Sidney - said to have been killed during the second War, lived "Glenaber", Blundell Avenue. *(Three other children - Albert, Wilfred and Bunty?) (Further suggestion that he died shortly after the war?)*

Lawrenson, Geofrey Charles, Lieutenant (S), Royal Naval Volunteer Reserve, H.M.S. *Excellent II.* Son of Captain Charles Joseph Frederic Lawrenson of Uplyme, Devon (formerly of "Hildene", Elmcroft Lane, Hightown.) *Commemorated on the Portsmouth Memorial. On 21 March 1944, while stationed at Portsmouth Barracks, Geofrey was lost overboard from a liberty boat, at night, when returning from an event aboard a vessel in the harbour. (One sister, Phyllis). (Also commemorated on the Merchant Taylor's School Memorial, Crosby).*

APPENDIX 4

The Hightown Club Roll of Honour

A framed illuminated scroll with a surround of photographs of the men who fell in WW1.

It is inscribed across the top:-

The HIGHTOWN CLUB

ROLL *of* HONOUR

1914 – 1918

(A watercolour scene of a cricket match in progress)

"Pro Patria Mori"

There follow 17 names & units of those who fell, arranged in 3 columns:-

Col. 1

Baines, Corpl. F.S. 6th Batt. King's L'pool Regt. Died of wounds 20.8.16.
Chaddock, H.B. 10th Batt. King's L'pool (Scottish) Regt. Killed in action 16.6.15.
Dawkins, Sergt. R.D. 10th Batt. King's L'pool (Scottish) Regt. Killed in action 16.6.15.
George, Pte. Frank 13th Batt. Cheshire Regt. Killed in action Aug. 1916.
Laslett, Lieut. H.G., M.C. Royal Field Artillery. Died of wounds 2.8.16.
Lawson, Capt. J. King's Liverpool Regiment.

Col. 2

McArdle, Corpl. R. 20th Batt. King's L'pool Regt. Killed in action 20.3.17.
Marsden, Sec.Lieut. H. King's L'pool Regt. Killed in action 1917.
Naylor, B.B. 1st King Edward's Horse. Killed in action 1917.
Nevin, Lieut. R.D. R.F.C. Killed in action 1918.
Rutter, Major E.F. East Lancashire Regt. Killed in action 22.5.15.
Thorp, F. 19th Batt. King's L'pool Regt. Killed in action 30.2.16.
M.A.

Col. 3

Vance, Lance cpl. A. 10th Batt. King's L'pool (Scottish) Regt. Killed in action 15.12.14.
Walker, Sergt. G.F. 2/10 Royal Scots. Killed in action Nov. 1918.
Weld Blundell, Lieut. R.S. 7th Batt. King's L'pool Regt. Accidentally killed 1.1.16.
White, Sec.Lieut. J.P. 10th Batt. King's L'pool (Scottish) Regt. Killed in action 16.6.15.
Wills, Sec.Lieut. J.G. R.F.A. Killed in action Sep. 27. 18.

Serving with His Majesty's Forces

There follow 3 columns of names & units:-

Col. 1

Allen, Lieut. Geo. 14th Batt. (Attd. 19th) King's L'pool Regt.
Ackerley, H.A. R.N.A.S.
Atkinson, W.R. R.G.A.
Blackledge, Sec.Lieut. R. 13th Batt. King's L'pool Regt.
Blake, Lieut. R.N.
Blumer, Pte. Francis. O.T.C.
Blundell, Capt. F.N. (Of Crosby) Lancs. Hussars.
* *Briggs, Sec.Lieut. H.* 6th Batt. King's L'pool Regt.
Breckell, Sec.Lieut. H.S. 17th Batt. King's L'pool Regt.
Broughton, B. Royal Naval Division.
Brown, G.E. 16th Batt. King's L'pool Regt.
Budden, W.B. R.F.A.
Byford, Lieut. Alan. Duke of Lancaster's Own Yeomanry.
Chisholm, J. Royal Naval Division.
Clayton, Capt. E. 20th Batt. Manchester Regt.
Cotton, Lieut. A.F. 10th Batt. King's L'pool (Scottish) Regt.
Concannon, Lt.Col. 7th Batt. King's L'pool Regt.
Davies, Capt. J.A. R.N.R.
Davies, C. R.G.A.
Dawkins, Sec.Lieut. J.R. 7th Dragoon Guards.
Derviche-Jones, Lieut.Col. A.D. D.S.O. M.C. 28th Batt. London Regt.
bb *Dorning. Capt. E.S.* 7th Batt. King's L'pool Regt.
Duncan, Major T.M. R.F.A.
Duxfield, R.J. 10th Batt. L'pool (Scottish) Regt. *[Word "King's" is missing]*
Fraser, Capt. G.W. Royal Engineers.

Col. 2

Garner, Lieut. J. Douglas. 1/4th Dorset Regt.
Gibson, Lieut. N. Inland Water Transport.
Gaukroger, L.Cpl. J.A. R.A.M.C.
Harrison, B. 10th Batt. King's L'pool (Scottish) Regt.
Haworth, Capt. R. A.S.C.
Hay, J.W. 4th Batt. East Kent Regt. (The Buffs)
Hazlewood, W.A. 7th Batt. King's L'pool Regt.
Henry, George. Duke of Lancaster's Own Yeomanry.
Hinton, G.M. H.A.C.
Holme, Sec.Lieut. J.O. Mongomeryshire Yeomanry.
Hopkinson, H. 10th Batt. King's L'pool (Scottish) Regt.
Hughes, Sec.Lieut. B.E.H. 10th Batt. Manchr. Regt.
Imlach, Capt. H.J. R.A.M.C.
Irving, Sergt. W.N. R.A.M.C.
Krohn, F. 17th Batt. King's L'pool Regt.
Lamont, Sec.Lieut. S.J. 4th Battery 1st (3) East Lancs. R.F.A.
Lewis, E. 6th Batt. King's L'pool Regt.
Lloyd, Sergt. J.B. Inns of Court O.T.C.
Lynch, Lieut. T. Massey. King's Own Royal Lancaster Regt.
Lowe, W. A.S.C.
Mantle, Sec.Lieut. R.L. South Lancs. Regt.
Marriott, Lieut-Col. 15th Batt. Royal Sussex Regt.
Matthews, M. R.F.A.
McAdam, J. 17th Batt. King's L'pool Regt.
McQueen, S.B. Inns of Court O.T.C.
Mees, Sec.Lieut. C.E. 17th Batt. King's L'pool Regt.

Col. 3

Murphy, A.L. 45th Anti-Aircraft Coy. R.G.A.
Murphy, Capt. E.P. 8th Batt. King's L'pool Regt.
Naylor, J.W. 1st King Edward's Horse.
Payne, Capt. A. West Lancs. R.F.A.
Raven, W.N. R.N.A.S.
Rimmer, Capt. E.J. Lancashire Fortress Royal Engineers.
Ridge, Lieut. F. Lancashire Fortress Royal Engineers.
Rogers, T. 10th Batt. King's L'pool (Scottish) Regt.
Rouch, Sec.Lieut. H.W. A.S.C.
Rush, Sapper T.H. Royal Engineers.
Rider, Bombr. D.D. 3/2 Lancs. R.G.A. (T.F.)
Smith, J. 17th Batt. King's L'pool Regt.
d *Smith, Canon Linton M. Chaplain D.S.O.* 17/20th Batt. King's L'pool Regt.
Sykes, Dr. A.B. Lieut. R.A.M.C.
* *Thraves, Sec.Lieut. F.* 17th Batt. King's L'pool Regt.
* *Turner, Sec.Lieut. H.* Lancashire Fusiliers.
Turner, Pte. D. Inns of Court O.T.C.
Tunnicliffe, Lieut. H.E. M.C. 1st Batt. South Wales Borderers (Attd. Brigade H.Q.)
Uren, H.J. O.C.B.
Van Eyck, Capt. E.C. R.A.M.C.
Walker, Major J. Lancashire Fusiliers.
Wall, Capt. R.D. 4th Coy. Machine Gun Corps.
Widdows, Lieut. J. 5th Batt. King's L'pool Regt.
Wilkinson, T.H. 18th Batt. King's L'pool Regt.
Wilson, A.H. 10th Batt. King's L'pool (Scottish) Regt.
Wright, C.W. Asst. Mechanic R.F.C.

Below these 3 columns is inscribed, in one line:-

* Wounded # Prisoner of War † Missing b Mentioned in Dispatches d Bar to Distinguished Service Order

---

Invalided out of Service or Discharged

There follow 6 groups of names & units in the pattern 1 4 2 6 5 3

Group 1.

Baines, J. S. 6th Batt. King's L'pool Regt.
Batchelor, Sergt. W.H. R.A.M.C.
Bennett, Lieut. S. West Yorks. Regt.

Group 2.

Brown, J.S. 10th Batt. King's L'pool (Scottish) Regt.
Chaddock, T.A. R.A.M.C.
Coote, Sec.Lieut. P.R. 9th Batt. King's L'pool.

Group 3.

Dumbell, Lieut. H.C. 3rd West Lancs. Brigade R.F.A. attached P.P.C.
Emmett, R. 6th Batt. King's L'pool Regt.
** *Hatch, L/Cpl. H.C.* 25th Batt. Manchester Regt.

Group 4.

Lightbound, Capt. Austin.	8th East Lancs. Regt.
Lees, Capt. R.	Duke of Lancaster's Own Yeomanry.
Lewis, Sergt. Wilfred.	6th Batt. King's L'pool Regt.

Group 5.

Marsh.	10th Batt. Liverpool (Scottish) Regt. *[Word "King's" is missing]*
Pearson, Reg.	Cambridge University O.T.C.
Russell, T.H. Junr.	18th Batt. King's L'pool Regt.

Group 6.

Reeves, Sergt. H.	6th King's L'pool Regt. *[Word "Batt." is missing]*
Rider, Cpl. W.W.H.	Tank Corps.
Swift, W.	17th Batt. King's L'pool Regt.
Townsend, J.W.	6th Batt. King's L'pool Regt.
Wishart, W.A.	10th Batt. King's L'pool (Scottish) Regt.

There are 6 photographs down each side and 5 across the bottom. They are named:-

Corpl. F.S. Baines	*H.B. Chaddock*
Sergt. R.D. Dawkins	*Pte. F. George*
Lieut. H.G. Laslett. M.C.	*Capt. J. Lawson*
Corpl. R. McArdle	*Sec.Lieut. H. Marsden*
B.B. Naylor	*Lieut. R.D. Nevin*
Major E.F. Rutter	*E.(?) Thorp M.A.*

L.Cpl. A. Vance *Lieut. R.S. Weld Blundell* *Sec.Lieut. J.G. Wills*

Sec.Lieut. J.P. White *Sergt. G.F. Walker*

APPENDIX 5
Hightown Club

Hightown Recreation Club was founded in 1906. Its first officers were: W.J. Blundell, President; T.H.Russell, Chairman; T.H.Russell Jnr, Secretary; D.N.Graham, Treasurer; G. Plummer Campbell & R. Sutton Pearson, Committee Members.

The first fixture the club played was in December 1906 – a soccer match played at the Yeomanry Field, which Hightown won. (The Yeomanry Field had been leased to the Duke of Lancaster's Own Imperial Yeomanry for ten years - in the first instance - at the turn of 19th / 20th century. A Crosby Herald report from 1901 describes a magnificent pavilion as well as a guardroom, a mess, a dining hall and several marquees. The field was adjacent to Sandy Lane.)

In 1907 "Recreation" was dropped from its title, and it became "Hightown Club", and 1907 is usually given as the year the club officially began. By that year there were thirty members and there was deemed to be sufficient interest to include cricket and tennis in the summer. To provide space for these sports the club obtained a lease of the present ground, from the Blundell Estate. Originally it was just a ploughed field, but it was levelled, and a cricket square and three tennis courts were created in time for the summer of 1908. In that year the Yeomanry Regiment decided to vacate their ground and dispose of their buildings, the latter were purchased by the club, and converted into a tennis pavilion and a cricket pavilion. The Crosby Herald in describing the new ground said: "It only remains for the club to go on as it has begun and its bright and prosperous future is assured."

During the 2nd World War the club was kept open. The Crosby Home Guard regularly played cricket there, while members of the Northern Cricket Club - who had had their ground taken over by the War Department - also made use of the club and were granted honorary membership.

One of the most noteworthy members of the club after the war was Philip Winter who was Captain of the cricket 1st XI for several seasons; he was also a County hockey player and honorary general secretary of the club for eighteen years. He and his late wife Audrey served the club well for many years in different capacities. Until very recently they still lived in Hightown (and proved to be a great help in compiling this edition of 'My Hightown').

The club celebrated its fiftieth anniversary in 1957 and this was marked by the gift of the Krohn Scoreboard handed over by Mrs Doris Krohn. Both Mrs Krohn's husband Leslie and her son Peter had been staunch supporters of the club.

Soccer was the first sport played by Hightown Club and for a while the Hightown team did well: after the 1st World War they joined the I Zingari League, playing against such teams as Marine F.C. and the Liverpool Police. In 1922 they won the I Zingari Challenge Cup beating Marine 2-0 in the final. However during the 1930s interest waned and the soccer team was disbanded. This was partly due to the increasing popularity of rugby, a section having been formed in 1924.

Cricket and hockey have proved to be enduringly popular. The men's and women's hockey teams have been particularly successful over the years, and many Hightown Club players have represented Lancashire and England; Colin Whalley, for instance, was part of the British hockey team that played at the Mexico Olympics in 1968. Squash was also added to the number of sports played at the club when courts were opened in June 1971. In fact the 1971 edition of the Hightown Club review could boast participation in ten different sports - however this list also included "One-Armed-Banditry".

APPENDIX 6
Fort Crosby

(i) Fort Crosby

Building at this site began in 1906. The Fort was headquarters for the Lancashire and Cheshire Heavy Brigade of the Royal Artillery, as well as for the Mersey and Barrow defences. After the 1st World War it was used as a training centre; there was a regular Major in command and about 40 gunners to man it. They also looked after the defences of Walney Island off Barrow-in-Furness. The Fort was never in action during the 2nd World War but examined shipping coming into the area. However the battery grew to include a well-dispersed system of searchlights, barracks and anti-aircraft guns.

After the war Fort Crosby was used to house German POWs; it also had a cinema which showed German and English films, and proved to be popular with local residents. Every Christmas the German POWs would put on a concert at the Industrial School.

A headline in the *Liverpool Echo* of May 1964 stated, "Fort Crosby to be demolished", but in fact it was not completely demolished until September 1967.

36. Fort Crosby, c1950

(ii) Fort Crosby : information from Kevin Bargen:

"Fort Crosby was situated on the coast amidst the sandhills half way between Hightown and Hall Road, it had its own railway crossing, Sniggery Crossing. It was built in 1906 to protect the Mersey estuary along with Fort Perch Rock at New Brighton. It had major gun emplacements facing out to sea, anti-aircraft guns and searchlights.

At the end of World War Two a German prison camp was built at the Fort, Camp 678; the prisoners were controlled by both British and Polish soldiers. The camp had a church, cinema, hospital and football pitch. The prisoners had left the camp by 1950 and the TA used Fort Crosby until 1954. Although the whole base closed in 1957 it wasn't finally dismantled and blown up until 1967.

The last Resident District Gunner at Fort Crosby was Sergeant Albert Bargen, he lived in the Fort with his family until 1957. His children Kevin and Elizabeth went to Little Crosby School, attended Our Lady's Church, Hightown and were active members of The Hightown Club."

37. Fort Crosby, March 1957

An officer from 253 Crane Operating Squadron, Royal Engineers, T.A., watches from the top of Fort Crosby as 14 pounds of gun cotton and 20 pounds of plastic explosive shatter an outlying concrete block-house. During the process of de-requisitioning the fort, demolition training was combined with destruction of part of the complex.

APPENDIX 7

The Truant School, Hightown

by Andrew Lee-Hart

The Truant School was a major feature of Hightown, and one of the first buildings in the village. Joe Bulman mentions it frequently; and it is interesting to note the awe and fear in which he and his contemporaries held it.

Background

Hightown Truant School was for truants from Liverpool (and later on further afield). It was only for truants rather than for other miscreants - special schools, such as Kirkdale Industrial School, were available for them.

The legislation that led to the creation of Truant Schools was the 1866 Industrial Schools Act. However it was the 1870 Education Act that brought the problem of truancy to the fore. This Act introduced elementary education for all children and instituted School Boards that were empowered to fill the gaps in the existing voluntary provision of elementary education.

Despite the 1870 Act many children still did not attend school. In the mid-1890s Sir John Gorst, Conservative Vice-President of the Education Council, told Parliament that a quarter of a century after the 1870 act there were "... nearly three-quarters of a million of children whose names ought to be on the books of some elementary school, and who do not appear at all ... Of those who are on the books of the elementary schools, nearly one-fifth are continually absent." (*A Social History of Education in England* by John Lawson p325)

Truant schools were one means by which School Boards tried to deal with this absenteeism, but these institutions were by no means universal. According to the Reformatory Inspections of 1889, there were only ten Truant Schools in England and Wales: as well as Hightown, they were in Brighton, Bristol, Fyfield (London), Kingston-upon-Hull, Plymouth, Sheffield, Swansea, Upton House (London) and Walthamstow. According to Radzinowitz (quoted in *History Today* June 2000 p27), by the eve of World War One there were twelve Truant Schools.

The *Encyclopedia Britannica* (1911 edition) said "The total admissions to truant schools in 1907 were 1,368 boys, the average length of detention was fourteen weeks and three days on first admission, seventeen weeks and five days on first re-admission and twenty three weeks six days on second re-admission. The total number of admissions into truant schools from 1878 to the end of 1907 was 44,315."

The local School Boards controlled Truant Schools. School Boards were made up of between five to fifteen elected members. All ratepayers could serve on School Boards or vote for members, including women. The School Boards were abolished by the 1902 Education Act, and the 120 county boroughs and counties were substituted in their place. These had oversight of all branches of education - elementary, secondary and technical. Thus the Truant School at Hightown would have been taken over by the Liverpool Education Committee in 1902.

Setting up the school

The Liverpool School Board set up Liverpool Truant School, Hightown. A report of the Special (Street Arab) Committee (8th March 1875) was presented to the Board on10th May 1875. Among its recommendations was the setting up of the Truant School. The report in many ways has modern resonance: "In dealing with children of this class, the Board has always experienced very great, and, until its recent action under the Industrial School Act, 1866, insuperable difficulties. The circumstances of some parents render it impossible for them to exercise the control over their children necessary to secure regular attendance at school. There are many other cases - difficult of detection - in which the excuse that the child is beyond parental control is made as a cloak to hide the parents' neglect."

On 11th October 1875 the General Purposes Committee recommended putting that part of the report dealing with Truant Schools into practice, stipulating that it was for boys only, and that Protestants and Roman Catholics should have separate religious exercises and instruction.

A month later, on 8th November, the General Purposes Committee recommended purchasing 27 Northumberland Terrace, Liverpool for the school. However this must have come to nothing because on 12th June 1876 the District Education Committee stated "...suitable premises for the truants' Industrial School have not yet been found..." and that the Sites and Building Committee be requested to obtain plans and estimates for the erection of a school to accommodate about sixty boys in each section.

On 10th October 1876, the Sites and Building Committee recommended that - subject to Home Office consent - they buy land in Hightown from Colonel Blundell for £500, for the Truants' Industrial School. The board applied to the Education Department for their recommendation to the Public Works Loan Commissioners of a loan to the amount of £9,960 to cover the expenses connected with the erection the school. A George Hayter was appointed as Clerk of the Works at a salary of £2 5s per week.

Once it had been built, children from other districts of Lancashire soon attended the Truant School; in June 1880 children from the District of Blackburn were to be received at the cost of 8s 6d per week. The School Board minutes of 4th November 1880 show children admitted from other districts for the same cost of accommodation.

Rules and regulations

Extracts from the *Rules for the Government of the Truants' School*, adopted by the Liverpool

School Board, 1st February 1883:

- The Truants' School placed under the management of a body of managers appointed by the Board... consisting of not more than eight gentlemen and four ladies, in addition to the chairmen of the District Education and Industrial Schools Committees, and the chairman and vice-chairman of the Board, ex officio.

- The residence of each section shall consist of the undermentioned officers:- a Superintendent, a Matron, a Visitor of Licensed Children, a Caretaker and Industrial Master, a Cook, a Laundress.

- Superintendent shall reside on the premises, and have sole charge of the school, and shall be responsible to the managers and the School Board for the good management thereof.

- Maximum salaries of the other resident officers :
  Visitor of Licensed Children £50 a year
  Caretaker and Industrial Master £45 a year
  Cook £20 a year
  Laundress £18 a year

(In 1876 the District Education Committee recommended that the Superintendents of the two sections (i.e. Protestant & Roman Catholic) should both be paid £120 a year.)

- The school is designed for the reception of about 80 children.

- Each child lodged in the school shall have a separate bed.

- All letters to or from the boys in the school shall be opened and read by the Superintendent, who may retain them if they appear to him to be unsuitable.

- Secular school instruction shall consist of reading, spelling, writing, arithmetic, music, and other fitting secular instruction.

- The industrial work shall consist of one or more of the following occupations: sack making, net making, wood chopping, and if possible, paper-bag making and printing, and match-box making - or of such other industrial occupations as the Board may from time to time consider practicable and desirable.

- Treatment of Children: Disciplinary Stage and Probationary Stage:

Disciplinary Stage - child 9 or over for four days on first occasion, fortnight on second or subsequent occasion, child over 12; one month on the third or on any subsequent occasion.

Boys shall sleep in separate bedrooms and do industrial work separately and in their own rooms, mingling with the rest of the inmates only at morning and evenings prayers, at lessons, and at meals.

Separate bedrooms shall open out of a corridor, shall be so placed as to be constantly under the supervision of some member of the school staff; shall have a grating through which light shall shine into the room all night from such corridor, and shall be provided with a bell communicating with the bedroom of the officer in charge.

In lieu of play the children shall be engaged in drill for not less than one hour and a half per day.

The boys shall be supplied with a sufficient amount of wholesome, but very plain food according to a diet to be fixed by the School Board.

Probationary stage - stage shall apply to all children under 9 years of age, and to such children above that age as have passed through the disciplinary stage.

In this stage the children shall be treated as in an ordinary industrial school, and subjected as much as possible to softening humanizing influences.

Boys in this stage shall be allowed not less than two hours daily for recreation and exercise at times to be fixed in the time table, and shall occasionally be taken out for exercise beyond the boundaries of the school, in charge of some of the officers thereof.

- Punishments by Superintendent only:

Forfeiture of rewards and privileges

Reduction in quantity or quality of food, but no boy shall be deprived of two meals in succession.

Moderate personal correction by whipping with a common school rod or cane to be inflicted only by the Superintendent, and not to exceed at any one time five strokes in the case of a boy under 9 years of age, or nine in the case of a boy above that age.

Confinement in his separate bedroom, in the case of a child in disciplinary stage, and in any other case, in a separate bedroom. Such confinement not to exceed, in the case of a child over 9 but under 12 years of age, 24 hours, or in the case of a child over 12 years of age, 36 hours. No child under 9 years shall be confined in a separate room.

- In the event of any boy making use of the greater liberty allowed in this stage to escape or attempt to escape from the school, he shall if above 9 years of age, on recapture or discovery, be whipped with a common school rod or cane by the Superintendent, the number of strokes not to exceed twelve, and be returned to the disciplinary stage for as long a period as in the case of a re-admission."

Latter days

The school was temporarily closed during the 1st World War but re-opened afterwards.

As Joe Bulman says, the Truant School changed its purpose on a number of occasions during his lifetime. At one time it was a Remand Home for 'backward' children. In 1936-37 the whole establishment transferred to Penketh near Warrington. It was remained open until 1962-63, then transferred to Port Dinorwic, in North Wales. The Hightown Truant School building was demolished shortly afterwards.

Chris Scott in her book *At Random in Hightown* also mentions the Truant School. She speculates that the school may have been built with bricks from the old Walton Gaol. She also says that during the 2nd World War "...children from Liverpool were evacuated to the Truant School (the Remand Home boys having been moved away by this time)."

The Truant School ensured a place for Hightown in educational history and was a feature of village life for many years. The building may have gone, but its memory lingers on.

38. Hightown Truant School
An early 20th century view

APPENDIX 8
PC Bond

PC Joseph Bond is famous in Hightown's history as the man who heroically fought the Crosby Lighthouse fire.

Joseph Bond hailed from Devon. Originally a soldier, he had joined the 1st Battalion, 13th Somerset Light Infantry in April 1874 and was stationed at Newry, Ireland, until 1st July 1874 when he was transferred to the 1st Battalion Royal Lancaster Regiment (King's Own), stationed at Fort Grange, Gosport. He embarked with the Battalion for Gibraltar on 26th September 1874 and was stationed there until 6th January 1879. The unit was sent to Jamaica, where he stayed until May 1882; he then embarked for England, arriving at Devonport in June. Bond took his discharge on 7th April 1886 after completing 12 years with the Colours.

After his career in the army, Joseph Bond joined the Lancashire County Police in June 1886 and was stationed at St. Helens; he transferred to St. Helens Borough Police the following year. He resigned in May 1890, rejoining the Lancashire County Police shortly afterwards, and was posted to the Bury Division until March 1892. He was then transferred to the Seaforth Division, and stationed at Hightown until December 1901 when he took over his last beat, in Blundellsands. He retired in September 1913.

At a presentation to mark his retirement, Sir William Scott Barrett, J.P. said of PC Bond "He was a strong believer in the old saying, 'Prevention is better than cure'. He thought he was doing his work much better if he kept people out of mischief than catching them after it was done."

Bond rendered excellent service during the lighthouse fire and the coroner's jury, in recording their verdict, made special mention of his work, and recommended that it should be noticed at Headquarters. As a consequence he was promoted to the Merit Class.

On 2nd February 1898 Thomas Bolton, a Hightown signalman, spotted a blaze in the general direction of the lighthouse and called out PC Bond at 4am. After visiting the lighthouse, which was well alight, Bond returned to the police station for ladders. Using them, he climbed into the upstairs room of the lighthouse, but there was no trace of the occupants. Charles Gaffney, postmaster and railway porter, assisted him.

The fire brigade from Crosby arrived at 6.30am but the building was beyond saving. The only supply of water was the domestic system, from a one-and-a-half inch pipe – insufficient for such a fierce blaze. By 9am the building was in ruins.

The only remains found of those occupants were charred bones. Those who perished in the fire were the lighthouse keeper Robert Buckley (48), his wife Ann (50) and a visitor, Mrs Alice Clements, a widow from Hoylake. A large collie dog belonging to the Buckleys also died in the blaze.

On the night in question there was a raging gale, and it is presumed that the window in the lamp room could have been blown in, thus causing the blaze.

BIBLIOGRAPHY

Ashton, W 'The Battle of Land & Sea' (Chapter on River Alt to Seaforth) 1909

Ashton, W 'Evolution of a Coastline' 1920

Atkinson, David & Houston, John (eds) 'The Sand Dunes of the Sefton Coast: proceedings of the Sefton Coast Research Seminar' 1991 ISBN 090636762X

Barrow, J P 'Crosby Lighthouse 1839-1898' 1955

Borough of Crosby 'Ministry of Town & Country Planning enquiry. Proposed housing development to the north end of Lower Alt Road & St. Stephen's Road, Hightown' 1946

'Directory of Waterloo, Blundellsands, Great Crosby & Seaforth' (various editions 1906 – 1929)

Farthing, Andrew 'Essential History of Little Crosby & Hightown' 1997

Foley, J W 'Submerged Forest at Hightown' 1952

Gresswell, R K 'Sandy Shores in South Lancashire: the geomorphology of South-West Lancashire' 1953

'Hightown Mission Church' (no date)

Maddock, Alison J 'The River Alt Level 1589-1779: a study of local watercourse management and flood prevention in the seventeenth and eighteenth centuries, with emphasis on the relationship between the communities of the level and their river' 1995

Mersey & Weaver River Authority 'River Alt Pumping Station' 1971

Scott, Chris 'At Random in Hightown' 1970

Sefton MBC 'Hightown Dunes' (no date)

Sefton MBC 'The Sefton Coast: a guide for schools' 1995

Sefton MBC 'The Sefton coast management plan 2nd Review 1997-2006: draft for consultation February 1997' 1997

Smith, Philip H 'The Sands of Time: an introduction to the sand dunes of the Sefton Coast' 1999 ISBN 1902700031

Taylor, Henry 'Ancient Crosses & Holy Wells of Lancashire with notes on pre-Reformation Churches & Monasteries' 1906

Tyrer, F & Miller, J A 'Notes on the History of Crosby & District' (no date)

Further information on P.C. Bond may be found in the Police Examination Book (PLA11/26) at the Lancashire Record Office, Preston

39. FUN 123

This photo was taken in June 1958 and shows Jim and Phyll Hinde getting ready for a wedding. Village Way now turns left beyond the school sign; Hillcrest Road is now where the school wall is on the photograph. Their car was a Triumph Roadster, a model produced between 1946 and 1949.

40. Aerial view of Hightown
Undated. It shows, among other things, the old level crossing over the railway line, the Truant School, the Hightown Hotel, School Road with Joe Bulman's house "The Luff", the village green and, on the extreme right, the War Memorial. (Reproduced courtesy of the Southport Visiter*)*